Gender, Development and Social Change

Series Editor
Wendy Harcourt
The International Institute of Social Studies
Erasmus University
The Hague, The Netherlands

The *Gender, Development and Social Change* series brings together path-breaking writing from gender scholars and activist researchers who are engaged in development as a process of transformation and change. The series pinpoints where gender and development analysis and practice are creating major 'change moments'. Multidisciplinary in scope, it features some of the most important and innovative gender perspectives on development knowledge, policy and social change. The distinctive feature of the series is its dual nature: to publish both scholarly research on key issues informing the gender and development agenda as well as featuring young scholars and activists' accounts of how gender analysis and practice is shaping political and social development processes. The authors aim to capture innovative thinking on a range of hot spot gender and development debates from women's lives on the margins to high level global politics. Each book pivots around a key 'social change' moment or process conceptually envisaged from an intersectional, gender and rights based approach to development.

More information about this series at
http://www.palgrave.com/gp/series/14999

Fatma Osman Ibnouf

War-Time Care Work and Peacebuilding in Africa

The Forgotten One

palgrave
macmillan

Fatma Osman Ibnouf
University of Khartoum
Khartoum, Sudan

Gender, Development and Social Change
ISBN 978-3-030-26194-8 ISBN 978-3-030-26195-5 (eBook)
https://doi.org/10.1007/978-3-030-26195-5

This Palgrave Macmillan imprint is published by the registered company Springer Nature Switzerland AG
The registered company address is: Gewerbestrasse 11, 6330 Cham, Switzerland

To women who work tirelessly to take care of family and others during and after armed conflict ... Caregivers who contribute to ensure the survival and safety of their family, and even their community under the dust of war ... Instead of qualifying them a leading voice in peacebuilding, women carework is often taken for granted

Preface

The challenges of arranging for care needs are particularly severe in the wartime and post-conflict situations where the need for care is escalating as a consequence of such crises. Care work is usually provided by women and is often taken for granted or remains unchallenged because it is perceived to be women's daily routine work and familial labour. This happens in normal times but what about the role of women as caregivers in the time of crises (e.g. violent armed conflict)? There is, however, a lack of data and information on the specificity of care work arrangements and the profile of women as caregivers in armed conflict and post-conflict situations. This book aims to provide critical reflection on the current under-researched topic; the link between wartime care work provision and peacebuilding. The policy rationale is to inform and support evidence-based decision-making for the peace-oriented stakeholders. Researching and understanding the lives and experiences women as caregivers in countries affected by armed conflict in Africa, especially in Darfur—western Sudan, presents significant contextual, conceptual and methodological challenges. Thus, there is the need to consider the conceptual framework and methodological approaches that would best convey the experiences and voices of the women in these contexts. Adopting a feminist perspective, especially being empathic of the complexities of the lives of the women, was valuable in navigating some of these challenges. A feminist perspective entails the consideration of women's subjectivities both in wartime and peacetime. It considers the different ways in which women conceive themselves, individually and in relation to others, and their roles in society at different times—during and after a war, especially as caregivers. The ethics of care is giving for expression to women in different parts of Africa that have not been listened to before.

Khartoum, Sudan Fatma Osman Ibnouf

Acknowledgements

First of all I would like to give a special word of thanks to Mr. Ayenka Franklin, indeed I am greatly indebted to and sincerely thank you Franklin, for editing this book. I would like to express my appreciation of the critical editing you made which for sure improved the quality of the book. This research was funded by a grant awarded to the researcher by African Peacebuilding Network (APN) Individual Research Grants 2016 and APN's Book Manuscript Completion Grant 2017. I am most grateful to the APN for its support. I would like first to express my sincere appreciation and gratitude to the APN manager Prof. Cyril Obi, Dr. Vivian Isaboke, and Ms. Jennifer Sherys-Rivet, the APN staff, lecturers, experts, and my fellow participants. I am feeling grateful to you all for making this experience a success. I would like to express my sincere gratitude and appreciation to Prof. Amy Niang, Department of International Relations University of the Witwatersrand for her help and guidance. Thank you also to Prof. Heidi Hudson, Director of the Centre for Africa Studies at the University of the Free State, South Africa for the unfailing support to complete this study. Thank you to my best friend Prof. Samia Satti who has been unconditionally supportive. The outmost gratitude goes to all the respondents that took part in this research and made it possible. Especially I want to thank the respondents from the five IDP camps for their time to contribute and share their stories and life experiences with me. Their inspiring contributions, sharing of unique perspectives and their warm, welcoming hospitality are valued and much appreciated. I hope my book will become an educational book for professionals everywhere, promote academic debates, dialogue with practitioners and peacebuilders, and eventually, transformation. I hope my book reach out even to the ordinary people of the IDP camps everywhere in Africa. I am most grateful to the APN's anonymous referees for their valuable inputs and comments on the book proposal. Thanks to my research assistants, Eltyb Ibnouf, Fatma Geeda, Nafisa, and Huwa Salih, for their dedicated work in gathering data under difficult field conditions. My fieldworks would not have been possible without the support of Dr. Nagla Mohamed Bashir, Director of the Peace Studies and Community Development Center, University of Nyala and Dr. Emad, the Center of Peace Studies & Community Development, Omdurman Islamic University Branch in El-Fashier, I am enormously thankful for their support and hospitality. I would like to extend my sincerest gratitude and appreciation to my husband Dr. Ali Humoud Ali, I am extremely thankful to you for your encouragement and unwavering support throughout this laborious journey. I am privileged to have you in my life. I would like to thank my brothers, sisters, nieces, and nephews for love, enthusiasm, and support in so many different ways. I would like to take this opportunity to extend my sincere thanks and appreciation to all who have contributed, in so many different ways, for what you did for me—friends, colleagues, and many others. To Ms. Samia Nihar, program manager at Development Studies and Research Institute, I greatly appreciate your help and support. Thank you to my daughter Dan for your love! I am so blessed to have you in my life, I love you. To the souls of my beloved parents Osman and Saeeda "My Lord have mercy on them, as they raised me when I was a child" and to the souls of my brothers Ibnouf and Mohammed, may mercy of Allah be upon them.

Above all, my special praise and thanks be to **Allah**, for **His** innumerable bounties.

Contents

Acronyms/Abbreviations

AIDS	Acquired Immune Deficiency Syndrome
AU	African Union
AWD	African Women's Decade
CEDAW	Convention on the Elimination of all forms of Discrimination against Women
CPA	Comprehensive Peace Agreement
CRC	Convention on the Rights of the Child
CSOs	Civil Society Organizations
CSW	Commission on the Status of Women
DPA	Darfur Peace Agreement
DRC	Democratic Republic of the Congo
FGM	Female Genital Mutilation
FHH	Female Headed Household
GBV	Gender Based Violence
GDP	Gross Domestic Product
GGGR	Global Gender Gap Report
GNP	Gross National Product
GOS	Government of Sudan
HCS	Household Care Survey
HIV	Human Immunodeficiency Virus
ICATUS	International Classification of Activities for Time Use Survey
IDPs	Internally Displaced Persons
ILO	International Labor Organization IDPs
INGOs	International Non-Governmental Organizations
MDGs	Millennium Development Goals
MGI	McKinsey Global Institute

NAPs	National Action Plans
NGOs	Non-Governmental Organizations
SDGs	Sustainable Development Goals
SPLA	Sudan People's Liberation Army
SSA	Sub-Saharan Africa
UN	United Nations
UNAMID	UN–AU Mission in Darfur
UNCDF	United Nations Capital Development Fund
UNDP	United Nations Development Programme
UNFPA	United Nations Fund for Population Activities
UNHCR	United Nations High Commissioner for Refugees
UNICEF	United Nations Children's Fund
UNIFEM	United Nations Development Fund for Women
UNSCR	United Nations Security Council Resolution
UNU	United Nations University
USIP	United States Institute of Peace
VAW	Violence Against Women
WASH	Water, Sanitation and Hygiene
WE-Care	Women's Economic Empowerment and Care
WHO	World Health Organization
WIDER	World Institute for Development Economics Research

List of Figures

CHAPTER 1

Introduction Researching Wartime Care Work in African Conflict Countries

1.1 Wartime Care Work and Women's Endurance

Care arrangements during wartime are complex and include a range of tasks that are essential for sustaining lives and the well-being of the family. Unpaid care provision, therefore, include all those functions performed by women as care providers during and after a conflict, in the absence of the basic support services and means of livelihood for sustenance. More significantly, unpaid care arrangement is the foundation that saves the lives of many in armed conflict and post-conflict circumstances of Darfur. Care responsibilities are still not equally shared between men and women in practice. The particular areas affected by the war in Darfur, especially the increase in the demand for care due to the obvious pressures that war puts on daily life. As the violent armed conflict in Darfur escalates, the need for care, both in quantitative (prevalence of disability and illness, injuries, and malnutrition, etc.) and in qualitative terms (care implies dealing with extreme emotional situations such as sexual violence, psychological trauma, and grief), becomes even more vital for the lives of people caught in the conflict. There have been no state-supported childcare systems (or even orphanages) during and after the war. Thus, women shoulder the burden of caring orphaned children. Besides the experience of the wartime suffering, women may be raped or may witness the rape of their beloved ones, daughters, sisters, mothers which may cause traumatizing social experiences for them.

F. O. Ibnouf, *War-Time Care Work and Peacebuilding in Africa*, Gender, Development and Social Change,
https://doi.org/10.1007/978-3-030-26195-5_1

This, in itself, is one of the ways women become entangled in social activities in wartime. The burden intensifies when rape victims give birth resulting from their abuse. Such women provide care for themselves and also support the provision of care for others with no support systems. Making care more overt would be key to ensuring greater sustainability of social security systems. There is also an economic argument that considers the importance of unpaid care work in post-conflict reconstruction strategy; it is necessarily to be attentive to issues of gender inequality on one hand, and the relationship between care work and the status of women in the labour market in conflict setting. Despite the research's limitation to Darfur, its scope can be extended to cover other war-affected regions of the African continent, for the reason that, problems in other regions affected by war in Africa share similar patterns.

The objective of this book is to ponder the implications of integrating wartime and post-war care work into peacebuilding theory and practice. It emphasizes the value of care provision in armed conflict and post-armed conflict situations for knowledge production on peacebuilding and to better inform policy and post-armed conflict reconstruction efforts. First, the book is an attempt to gain a more nuanced understanding of an often forgotten and marginalized aspect of armed conflicts, namely the everyday structures that sustain lives during crises and periods of instability. Second, the importance of this publication lies in enhancing the understanding of the critical place that unpaid care work can be made to occupy in peacebuilding processes. Third, the book endeavours to show the lack of recognition for care work in armed conflict and the impact this disregard has on prevalent debates and strategies in peacebuilding frameworks. Fourth, it seeks to emphasize the importance of recognizing women as valid protagonists in post-conflict peace processes, as it is women who often take on the responsibility to sustain life during and after the armed conflict. This is not only a question of justice for people entangled in armed conflicts or to examine the importance of care work for people experiencing armed conflict as part of everyday life. It is also a question of adding a specific category of knowledge producers into peace and conflict studies.

Peacebuilding still lacks important elements necessary for understanding its reality, which can be viewed from different perspectives. To inscribe unpaid care work arrangements in wartime and post-conflict scholarship on peacebuilding and security studies, a better approach should investigate the challenge of armed conflicts starting from the reality in the grounds that communities affected by war have a responsibility to build the peace. Further, there is a need to change scholarly and policy thinking on armed conflict configurations and this means among other things to take into account the complexity of non-combatant structures of solidarity, care, and community order. This requires the inclusion of women's wartime experiences, especially as caregivers/providers, which is crucial in peacebuilding. All armed conflicts are highly contextual and merit a thorough analysis which can produce a strategy that makes the most of existing valued stakeholders, women as caregivers in this case because they have been at the forefront of violent conflict and provided daily needs for their families. Therefore, there is a need for possible ways to consider unpaid care provisions during and after war as a critical dimension of a broader process of peacebuilding and reconstruction. This dimension is sorely overlooked in many peacebuilding efforts. Wartime care work can be a fundamental issue in peacebuilding, since care is central to the survival of people during a war and in refugee crisis and internal displacements as well. Survival and well-being are grounded in the understanding of peace. Peace is not only the absence of war, but the enjoyment of economic and social justice, and the entire range of human rights within society.

Many African countries have been plagued by armed conflicts for decades. Darfur has raged in armed conflict since 2003, forcing more than two million people from their homes. Women make up the majority of the internally displaced persons (IDPs) according to the roughly estimation of the UN humanitarian community. At the same time, women are powerful agents of peace and their efforts need recognition, support, and exposure. They help sustain social well-being through care provisions and also contribute to the social security system and solidarity which are strong instruments in relation to gender and armed conflict transformation. Wartime care provision aims to respond to the challenges of the neediest in such a specific context. The unvalued contribution of women is such that any reasonable calculation of their unpaid work would lead to a fundamental change in the context in which peace and security decision-making are framed. An understanding of the context of women's unpaid care provision in peacebuilding would help to put in place strategies that would sustain life and a lasting peace. A focus on care would be a key to ensuring greater sustainability of social security systems. It is now time to think of different ways to break the concrete ceiling to build a lasting and sustainable peace. Positive peace demands a rethinking of how wartime caregiving contributes to the survival of war-affected populations, while at the same time challenging the marginalization of the voices of women as caregivers in building peace.

This book puts forward the argument that the proximity of women to care in peacebuilding means that they value life that their commitment to establish peace is firm, informed and active. The actions of women as peacebuilders start from their everyday caregiving and the concern they establish to manage the survival and safety of their family, and even their community. The idea is not to deify women's sacrificial defiance, but to reclaim the value of women's commitment to life and make it everyone's commitment. This work also ascertains that the critical role that women play through their care work should not only be recognized, it should in fact qualify them as leading actors in peacebuilding processes. On the other hand, to what extent can unpaid care work arrangements be incorporated within the post-armed conflict reconstruction strategies? How could this be done? The State needs to respond to women's burden of unpaid care work by re-conceptualizing the four principles of care work in light of potential contribution to peacebuilding and post-armed conflict reconstruction. The four principles of unpaid care work are recognition, reduction, redistribution, and representation: *recognition* through appropriate measurement and recognition of wartime care as an essential element of survival and well-being; *reduction* by investing in social infrastructure, basic services and lessening the burden of unpaid care; *redistribution* guided by prioritizing the goal of gender equality through encouraging equality in intra-household allocation and equal meaningful sharing of care responsibility in addition to the state sharing in the care responsibility through provision of care services; *representation* by increasing equal participation of men and women in institutional processes, practices, and policies, including peace negotiations, *representing* the voices and concerns of women as caregivers in the peace and decision-making processes at large. The four principles seem to have been almost forgotten in the world of conventional unpaid care work. The inclusion of women as caregivers/providers during war and its aftermath can be positive because it means that more experiences will be reflected in the peace realm. Thus, the ultimate argument is that care work makes more salient the plurality of experiences, perspectives, and input in peacebuilding frameworks. The recognition of this key aspect will generate substantial benefits including the enhancement of gender equality and the empowerment of women. More generally, it would make vital contributions to the literature on peacebuilding, unpaid care work, post-conflict reconstruction studies, and humanitarian action.

In the Darfur, as well as in other war-affected regions in Africa, the feminist ethics of care provides a suitable theoretical approach for research and post-armed conflict peacebuilding for four reasons:

1. Women bear the burden of unpaid care work, responding to the cultural expectations of their social positions and responsibilities. The feminist ethics of care approach brings to light the challenges women caregivers face and contributes to broaden the thinking on the link between regular care work and wartime care work. It opens up possibilities to address the subordination of women, the disproportionately higher level of unpaid care work they provide, and how it impacts them. Thus, practical recommendations are made that peace should be built in a manner that respects "the principles of unpaid care work", namely, recognition, reduction, redistribution, and representation.
2. A feminist approach provides an effective means to deal with a common devaluation of caring arrangements. It insists on the importance of the role of women in unpaid care work arrangement averting the disregarded.
3. The approach recognizes that the voices of women as caregivers have been ignored in the conception and implementation of peacebuilding processes. Therefore, it can be argued that the critical role women play through their care work qualifies them as leading actors in peacebuilding.
4. It offers useful insights into assessing whether peacebuilding frameworks sufficiently recognize the practical realities of the lives of women, especially the challenges of providing care in and out of armed conflict. It would enable such frameworks to adequately address gender equality and gender-justice, and to advance women's human rights concerns and access to justice.

Based on the aforementioned, there is a need to change our collective thinking understanding of the realities of conflict by focusing on actors on the ground, directly involved in its various aspects rather than just taking an expert's point of view which may be distant from the reality on the ground. The norm of peace itself has been changed and peace is no longer the mere absence of violence. Peace now encompasses, among others, ensuring human security, social justice, and equality. Therefore, there is a need to diverge from merely considering the pre-determined standards of peacebuilding, and to start from the perspective of what would best serve the needs on the ground of the affected community. The scope of this book offers an overview of the possible ways to consider unpaid care arrangements in wartime and aftermath as critical dimensions of a broader process of the peacebuilding and the post-conflict reconstruction strategy. Women as caregivers during and after wartime possess unique lifesaving experiences, and thus, a need for their voices to reach the peace table. The book also seeks to contribute to the current global debates on why more women are needed in peacebuilding processes and post-conflict reconstruction. It concludes with the implications and lessons drawn from the Darfur case study which can be applicable to other conflict zones in Africa.

1.2 Book Outline

This book is structured along the main themes, each of which is discussed in turn. It is divided into seven chapters, each of which comprises sections. Each section discusses key themes and issues relevant to the topic of the chapter. An abstract at the beginning of each chapter serves as a summary for that chapter. The book is organized as follows: This chapter introduces and gives a detailed explanation of the book's objectives and arguments. Chapter 2 gives the rationale of the study. It further provides a background and overview information of armed conflicts in Africa in general and Darfur in particular, including the cost of human life in armed conflict. This is followed by an overview of the impact of armed conflict on women. Chapter 3 reviews the relevant literature on unpaid care work. Given the obscurity of care work in armed conflict studies, the literature review is not just about revealing an important gap in conflict studies but more about showing how this obscurity affects the nature and the quality of recommendations formulated by scholars in this field of studies with regard to grassroots involvement on peace building strategy, and the treatment, more broadly, of war victims as human beings with considerable agencies. Chapter 4 is divided into two parts. The first part conceptualizes the notion of unpaid care work by looking carefully at concepts such as "care", "caregiving" and "burden of care". It also explores care needs and provision. For the purpose of this study, care work includes all those functions performed by women as caregivers/providers during wartime and in the post-armed conflict stage. The second part begins by making explicit the theoretical framework. The feminist ethics of care provides a suitable theoretical approach for this study. Unpaid care work done by women during and after wartime should be of particular concern to feminists. Ethical responsibilities to practical care work contribute to ensuring survival and well-being of the family and the community. Finally, the chapter describes the research approach employed in Darfur. Chapter 5 presents the findings of the empirical study—the lived experiences of caregivers both during and after armed conflict. The chapter poses and answers the fundamental questions it presents on care work arrangements during wartime and how it is provided after war in Darfur. It analyses the mechanisms of survival and the operations of care deployed by women in everyday settings during and after a war. This chapter further discusses these findings in light of the position of women in peacebuilding and reconstruction strategies. Chapter 6 illustrates care practices during and after war that reflect the gendered division of labour. This chapter sheds light on wartime care work and "Gender Justice". Caregiving is articulated as a woman's responsibility which has consequences on gender inequality. The discussions offered have a wider policy implication, in peacebuilding and reconstruction strategies. This chapter tackles the contribution of unpaid care work to the building of peace and it tries to answer questions such as why more women are needed in the peacebuilding processes. The chapter is to consider how rethinking peacebuilding as "must know and practised" processes when looking through the lens of wartime care work arrangement. Chapter 7 concludes with a discussion of the most salient points raised by this book: make the voices of women as caregivers heard during and after wars. The chapter contains the concluding remarks, lessons learned from the study, relevant policy aspects of the study, and it articulates a number of key recommendations.

For further resource materials, there is a comprehensive list of books and relevant academic journals. A complete list of bibliographies is provided for all sources cited in the text, and are appeared at the end of each chapter. Chapter endnotes displayed at the end of the chapter on which a note is made.

Notes

It should be noted that caregivers and care providers were used interchangeably in this book. "Care" is used throughout the book as a synonym for caregiving, care-providing, caring, and care work—the term used matches that are used in the literature which have been reviewed. Conflict (armed conflict, violent conflict) and war are used interchangeably in this book, even though their meanings are not identical. In this study conflict refers to mainly armed conflict, therefore armed conflict and war are considered synonymous because they both refer to civil strife, internal conflicts, deadly and violent conflicts—it refers to the fighting between Sudan's government forces and rebel groups in Darfur. Post-conflict and aftermath of conflict were used interchangeably in this book.

CHAPTER 2

Background and Overview

2.1 Why Is Wartime Care Work Needs to Be Researched

Conflict does not discriminate between genders. During and after war, men and women play different roles, have different needs and priorities, and face different constraints. Caregiving and household chores are gendered activities, with most (if not all) of the responsibilities pertained to women. Thus, women are the most burdened with care work. Unpaid care work by women during and after a war tends to be perceived merely as an extension of their "regular" household duties. In areas affected by war, there is an increase in the demand for care due to the pressures that war puts on daily life. In situations where women are the ones who need to receive care, limited or no access to care services is a problem, and they carry the burden. Despite the prevalence of civil wars and armed conflicts in many parts of Africa, little is known about wartime care work arrangements. Research conducted on the everyday lives of women and unpaid care work especially in war-affected areas, have significance in conveying the voices of the unheard and often marginalized in peace work. This study portrays the reality of wartime caregiving, the specific care arrangement experiences women have faced in dealing with sustaining lives during a conflict and in post-conflict situations. That is, to explore the ability of a woman to arrange available meagre resources so as to provide care for her family during wartime and to highlight the

F. O. Ibnouf, *War-Time Care Work and Peacebuilding in Africa*, Gender, Development and Social Change,
https://doi.org/10.1007/978-3-030-26195-5_2

complexities and challenges associated with women's responses to such situations. It also provides a critical reflection on the current under-researched topic: the link between wartime care work arrangements and peacebuilding. This will inform and support evidence-based decision-making for the peace-oriented stakeholders. These objectives not only bring to light the unpaid care work arrangement in armed conflict situations, but challenge peacebuilding stakeholders to think about the obvious ways in which care work arrangements by women during wartime can unintentionally contribute to the peacebuilding and human security. It is important to also recognize the role of women in wartime care work so as to adopt appropriate responses to their needs and priorities accordingly and to employ it as a basis for the provision of support programs and services in post-conflict situations.

Another important factor that has NOT been much thought is how armed conflict impacts care work arrangements as a whole. There exists little or no systematic and comprehensive analysis on care work. Care work is mentioned here and there when dealing with other topics (armed conflict and health, women's role in the post-armed conflict, etc.), but not as the main topic. Women are involved in the everyday activities of struggling for the survival of their family during war. Hence, care work arrangement is critical to the day-to-day survival and well-being of people during war as they try to maintain their livelihoods under unfavourable conditions. These points beg the questions: Is there an increase in the "quality" and "quantity" of care during conflict? Does caregiving in armed conflict imply an extra burden of dealing with emotionally extreme situations? Does new care need such as reproductive health care go unnoticed? Care needs increase due to higher prevalence of disability, psychological trauma, and illnesses such as HIV/AIDS, among others. Also arduous care is needed by women who become mothers as a consequence of rape. Despite the difficulties involved in the daily care work arrangement by women, neither the state nor the policy makers properly understand how much this care work benefits their families and also how much it costs them personally. These points not only shed light on wartime caregiving, but also highlights the under representation of women in peace processes, this disadvantage for women is a situation attributable to stereotypical gender norms that peacebuilding is male domains. Nonetheless, the lack of data has been a crucial obstruction to the integration of wartime care work in the peacebuilding agenda.

This work attempts to bridge this gap through the collection of primary data from the war-affected area—Darfur.

Wartime care arrangement is meant to respond to the challenges of neediest of the specific conflict context. In normal times, an individual's need for care determines the level of care provided, but is it the same in wartime or at least in some parts of Africa, afflicted armed conflict? A critical question is whether unusual or urgent care needs arise in and out of wartime requiring intensive responses, such as with high incidence of disability, causalities, psychological trauma, and deliveries of new born. The balance between care needs and care provided by the state, NGOs, CSOs is inadequate and therefore it can be said that conflict goes hand in hand with "care crisis". If so, is this what happens if women do not provide care and support for their family during and after war? A number of studies affirm that it is in fact women who play the key role in supporting families in times of conflict (see for example, Arostegui 2013). This means women as caregivers attempt to solve the crisis of care that is most sorely needed. During wartime, women caregivers play a unique role by responding to the growing demand for emergencies care needs. Given the already limited (or lack of) basic services, wartime care work can be seen as a "*costless* and *effective response*" to humanitarian needs by using limited available materials and skills. Thus, women as caregivers are in a privileged position to defend peace. The prospects for sustainable peace can be greatly improved by tapping into women's understanding of the challenges faced by their families and communities (civilians) and their insights into the most effective ways to respond to their care needs. How best can this "*costless* and *effective response*" be linked to the overall peace-building strategic framework?

The perpetual state of armed conflict has necessarily affected the roles that men and women have taken on. Broadly, men have adopted the role of combatants. They sometimes fled the situation, got conscripted, wounded, detained, or even killed. On the other hand, women have had to maintain peaceful homes by increasing the scale of their caregiving activities for independents and the community, which is what women often do without being asked. Armed conflict breaks down economic and social structures and this often results in an increased burden on women both during and after armed conflict. The caregiving is a growing social problem left for women during and the aftermath of war. Furthermore, during war and even after war, there are no public services and social networks are broken down. This increases the burden on women with round-the-clock caregiving responsibilities. This contribution of women leads to a fundamental change in the context in which peace and security decision-making are framed. Accounting for unpaid care work in wartime and its aftermath is the missing link that influences the achievement of lasting sustainable peace. Making wartime care work more visible would be a key to ensuring greater sustainability of social security systems. Holding women's experience up to the light is crucial because without doing this, we cannot fully understand shifting gender identities, roles, and power relationships in situations of conflict (Thompson 2006).

2.2 A Brief Overview of Conflict in African Context

In general, since their independence, most African countries have been continuously affected by armed conflicts. Though these conflicts are within national borders, they are however influenced by external interferences. Neighbouring countries also always play active roles in internal armed conflicts. Since the 1960s, a series of civil wars have played out on the African continent. Examples include Sudan, Chad, Angola, Liberia, Nigeria, Somalia, and Burundi, Rwanda, and Sierra Leone (Aremu 2010). African countries have experienced more than thirty wars since 1970, and some have been quite prolonged such as the wars in Angola, Mozambique, and Sudan, and most of these armed conflicts are fought within national borders (Akinboade 2005: 260). More than half of all African countries have experienced at least a year of armed conflict during the past three decades "African casualties of conflict exceed those of all other regions combined" (Venkatasawmy 2015: 26). Since the late 1980s, indeed, Africa is experiencing an increased rate in the number of conflicts than other regions and currently has the highest number of ongoing conflicts (Jackson 2002). Half of Africa's states are in conflict, affecting 20% of the continent's population. In mid-2001, serious internal conflict continued in Algeria, Western Sahara, Sudan, Chad, Somalia, Sierra Leone, Senegal, Guinea, Liberia, Congo-Brazzaville, Democratic Republic of Congo, Rwanda, Burundi, Uganda, Angola, and Nigeria (ibid.). These conflicts have complex root causes and severe consequences. They continue to undermine human security, rights, and human development. While the direct consequences of conflict are bad, the indirect consequences are much worse (Gates et al. 2012: 1720).

The consequences of civil wars and armed conflicts for civilians are substantial. War kills, but the consequences extend far beyond direct deaths, social, political, and economic institutions are indelibly harmed (Gates et al. 2012: 1713). The lives of millions of civilians have been devastated; their settlements disrupted which leads to an increase in internal displacements. War causes displacement, institutional breakdown, psychological damage, physical suffering, economic collapse, and myriad other harms (Berry 2015). While detailed estimates do not exist for the armed conflicts in Côte d'Ivoire, Sudan, and Somalia, among other places clearly, they have all exacted a terrible human toll (Williams 2008: 309). Civil wars kill people directly and immediately, destroy property, disrupt economic activity, and divert resources from health care (Ghobarah et al. 2004: 869). Crime and homicide rates rise in wars and may remain high afterwards in a culture accustomed to violence, and many of these effects last for years after the fighting (ibid.). Davis and Kuritsky (2002 cited in Ghobarah et al. 2004: 869) report that severe military armed conflict in sub-Saharan Africa (SSA) cut life expectancy by more than two years and raised infant mortality by 12 per thousand. The United Nations Security Council has expressed concerns that civilians, particularly women and children, account for the vast majority of those adversely affected by armed conflict. They make up most of the refugees and internally displaced persons (IDPs), and are increasingly targeted by combatants and armed elements. The indirect effects of conflict are likely to be much greater than the direct effects as civil wars displace large populations, and their temporary accommodation often exposes them to new risk factors (Gates et al. 2012). Many of these effects last for years after the fighting (Ghobarah et al. 2004: 869).

Men, women, boys, and girls are all victims of violent armed conflict (suffering tremendous pain), as they are members of the same families and communities. However, this "victimhood" takes different forms and gender is one of the influencing dimensions. Human Security Report (2005) states, "with the critically important exception of sexual violence, there is considerable evidence to suggest that men are more vulnerable to the major impacts of armed conflict. They are more likely to die on the battlefield, and are also more likely to be victims of collateral damage". Men are in many conflict zones targeted through their women. They may be to watch the rape of their wives and daughters. For instance, women were raped in front of their husbands, children, and compatriots during the Mozambique civil war—from 1977 to

1992 (Sideris 2003). Men and boys are forcibly recruited into fighting. They are also targets of gender- and sex-based violence. As indicated by Richards (2014: 322), there is a nasty concoction of forced, coerced conscription into an armed conflict that permeates both children and adults in the Democratic Republic of the Congo (DRC). Forced recruitment is most likely to occur when non-state armed groups experience manpower deficits and when accountability is low (ibid.). There has been growing concern on sexual violence against men that occurs in violent armed conflicts. For example, in the eastern DRC, a population-based survey found that almost one quarter of men (23.6%) had experienced sexual violence and in Liberia, a population-based survey unveiled that one-third (32.6%) of former male combatants reported experiencing sexual violence (Chynoweth et al. 2017). It is well recognized that women bear a disproportionate brunt of armed conflict, even though in most cases they are not directly engaged in fighting. A number of studies based in different parts of Africa have come to the same conclusion; armed conflict increases women's and girls' vulnerability to sexual violence, rape, and other forms of war crimes (see for example, Ferris 2007 in Liberia, Guinea, and Sierra Leone; Newbury and Baldwin 2001 in Rwanda). It is estimated that up to five thousand have been born as a result of rape during the genocide in Rwanda (Newbury and Baldwin 2001: 31). Wartime rape is a uniquely African issue, the DRC, for example, has been repeatedly called the rape capital of the world, and many recent high-profile cases of widespread wartime rape have occurred in SSA countries, including Liberia and Sierra Leone (Cohen et al. 2013). In the case of Mozambique, women constitute the large majority of victims of sexual violence (Sideris 2003). Because many women serve as caretakers of others, the impact of sexual violence during armed conflict extends beyond individual victims to their families and communities (Akinsulure-Smith 2014: 679).

Due to the outbreak and prolongation of violent conflicts, population displacement has grown in size and complexity over the past two decades (UNHCR 2017).[1] Africa is the continent with the largest number of internally displaced persons in the world (IDPs)[2] and IDPs are likely to rise. Africa hosts over one-third of the world's forcibly displaced people. 15 million people are IDPs in Africa, and 9 of the 24 countries with the highest rate of displacement are African (Eweka and Olusegun 2016). Nonetheless, most of these figures are estimates and projections. The figures refer only to those displaced by conflict and human rights violations

(Ferris 2012). Nigeria tops the list of the first three countries with the largest population of IDPs in Africa, followed by the Democratic Republic of Congo and Sudan, respectively (Eweka and Olusegun 2016). Although the numbers of internally displaced people vary from one African country to another, however, it has become clear that many African countries will be faced with the challenge of dealing with relatively sizeable groups of refugee migrants from countries affected by conflict. Women are often placed at the heart of the conflict. They constitute the majority of the forcefully displaced as they are non-combatant. The experiences of displaced persons (mostly women and children) are less frequently recognized and addressed. It is well-known that the longer displacement lasts, the more difficult it is to find sustainable solutions (Ferris 2012). The displacement situation demands a new approach that goes beyond humanitarian action to address the causes and long-term implications of internal displacements in Africa. Many questions on this issue remain unanswered. Have African governments altered their development and social policies in response to IDPs and refugee situation? The displacement has disproportionately affected women and their children. Where displacement becomes protracted, with no end in sight, displaced women struggle to make ends meet, particularly with lack of state support and with little or no response from humanitarian agencies.

2.3 The Context Darfur—Western Sudan

Since it gained its independence in 1956, Sudan has experienced and continues to suffer from internal conflicts especially in the following zones: Southern Sudan seceded from Sudan in 2011 as a consequence of conflict; there has been conflict in Nuba Mountains, Blue Nile, Eastern Sudan, Kordofan, and Darfur. The internal civil war remains the dominant cause of socio-political instability in the nation. Sudan like many African countries is multi-ethnic. There are multiple causes of internal violent conflict. The fight over natural resources predominantly land and water cause environmental hazards, economic issues. Historical factors are among the complex causes of armed conflict in many African countries. As a matter of fact, in Sudan like in many African countries, there are often armed conflicts between sedentary farmers and nomadic herdsmen over natural pasture and water, especially during the seasonal movements of herdsmen in search of water and pasture (see for example, in Sudan Abdul-Jalil 2008; in Nigeria Ajibo 2018). As Elbadawi and

Sambanis (2000) state "the relatively higher prevalence of war in Africa is not due to the ethno-linguistic fragmentation of its countries, but rather to high levels of poverty, failed political institutions, and economic dependence on natural resources".

Darfur occupies the far west of Sudan (see Fig. 2.1 the Map of Darfur of western Sudan) and shares international borders with four countries: Libya Chad, Central African Republic, and South Sudan. Darfur is the largest and most densely populated regions in Sudan, Sudan being one of largest countries in Africa. Darfur means "*land of the Fur*"; Fur is the largest ethnic group in the region (Ali 2014). Darfur is made up of diverse ethnic groups with shared commonalities including religion (Islam), a patriarchal culture, among others. In fact ethnically diverse

Fig. 2.1 The map of Darfur of western Sudan (*Source* CIA World Factbook)

developing countries feature prominently on the list of countries that have suffered from civil war and insurgency in recent decades according to Sriskandarajah (2005 cited in Venkatasawmy 2015: 31). The long duration of the conflict in Darfur by any means, remains an imperative problem. Different interrelated factors constitute the root causes of the conflict. The conflict started as a resource-based dispute between herdsmen and farmers before transforming into a full-blown war that has claimed over 200,000 lives and rendered over a million people homeless (FEWS-NET 2007 cited in Adisa and Adekunle 2010). From the mid-1980s Darfur witnessed a gradual increase in armed confrontation between various groups, the Fur against the largest nomadic group—the Arabs (janjaweed) (Abdul-Jalil 2008). This led to the end of peaceful pattern of complementary coexistence that characterized the relationship between the two sides for decades (ibid.). Furthermore, neighbouring countries engaged in armed conflicts and civil wars—Chad, Central Africa, and Libya helped fuelled the violence in Darfur. Still, factors like unemployment and poverty lured people into taking up arms. The vulnerable groups, groups that felt they have been unjustly treated, resorted to armed confrontation in an attempt to improve their situation. Thus, since 2006 the rebel groups in Darfur have been spectacularly fragmented, particularly along ethnic lines (Tanner and Tubiana 2007).

The foreseeable human consequence of armed conflict Darfur will be further displacement, family separation, and suffering for Darfurian people. Moreover, conflict cuts off people from their wider social systems and support networks. Armed conflict in Darfur offers so many insights into conflict analysis, peacemaking, and the difficulties associated with protracted (long-lasting) armed conflicts. The government of Sudan exerts great efforts to achieve peace as a prerequisite for the realization of other development programs. The different protagonists in Darfur have signed a series of ceasefire agreements to enable humanitarian access and ensure the security of personnel, but have frequently broken them. Intended to address the causes of the conflict, the Darfur Peace Agreement (DPA) contains provisions on power-sharing, political representation, wealth sharing and compensation for the victims of the conflict, ceasefire arrangements and long-term security issues, and a Darfur–Darfur Dialogue and Consultation designed to facilitate local dialogue and reconciliation (De Waal 2006 cited in Nathan 2006). On the contrary, continued violence in Darfur entails the DPA has heightened the conflict as a direct result of its shortcomings. Nonetheless, there is still a great deal of optimism among Darfurian people on the potential for building a lasting peace.

Armed conflict in Darfur negatively affects its people. Many are exposed to grave violation of human rights and social trauma. Hundreds of thousands of people have been killed, many have their family members unaccounted for, destruction of infrastructure, and more than two million are still living in IDPs camps. Looting, rape, and mass killings have continued, displacing 2.4 million people to refugee camps in Darfur and another 250,000 to camps in Chad (Leander and van Munster 2007). However, the true total is still unknown because some abandoned their own villages in search of protection and the prospect for better livelihoods in urban areas and the outskirts of cities. Despite this huge exodus, there is no systematic registration of displacement outside of camps for those who settle in provisional camps in rural and urban areas. Violence continues flare in the Jebel Marra area, which located in the centre of the Darfur; it has driven more and more people out of their homes. The lack of accurate statistics made it challenging to ascertain the proportion of displaced persons in any given IDPs camps. New IDPs arrive in the IDP camps whenever a new crisis erupts in the region. Behind these numbers lie the blighted lives of people affected by ongoing armed conflict in Darfur. Displacement affects adversely the economic, educational, social, health, and almost all aspects of the lives of every displaced person. Roughly three-quarters of the IDPs are women and children. The consequences of armed conflict for men and women in the Darfur region have been multifaceted. Men and women play different roles and experience differing realities. Most of those who are killed, wounded, or missing in war are men, while women are at risk of being raped, sexually assaulted, and experience gender-based crimes. Women are also excluded from basic care services. Armed conflict also paves the way for child marriages, domestic violence, maternal and infant deaths, poverty, social insecurity, and exploitation. Although both men and women share similar challenges when displaced, women also face challenges that are conditioned by social roles and their status as caregivers/providers. The challenging power of the internalization of the patriarchal culture emphasizes that the responsibility of care work and household activities often lies in women. Even religion (Islam) is mainly viewed and interpreted through a cultural lens that is already patriarchal. Thus, women are (in the longer term) potentially impacted more by conflict.

These challenges overwhelmed the voice of women caregivers in peacebuilding and reconstruction processes.

2.4 The Impact of Violent Conflict on Women—An Overview

In 2013, the United Nations Security Council held a day-long debate looking at the effects of war and conflict on women. In a press release, it stated, "Women and girls suffered disproportionately during and after war, as existing inequalities were magnified and social networks broke down, making them more vulnerable to sexual violence and exploitation". The UNSC has entirely unremarked on the everyday realities women as caregivers encounter during war; the vivid reality about the burden war places on women as they try tonsure the day-to-day survival amidst the violence and suffering. There is a broad literature on the negative direct and indirect impacts of violent armed conflict on women and the violation of their rights in post-conflict states (see for example, Bouta et al. 2005; Buvinic et al. 2013). However, the review of the literature on the impact of armed conflicts on women finds three fairly separate bodies of literature: the impact of armed conflict on changing gender roles and relations, women-headed households and post-armed conflict situations, and gender inequality and sexual violence used as a weapon of war. These three major areas of study are relevant in attaining the purpose of this book. The roles of women change in the household and in the community during and after violent conflicts. They occupy multiple roles and so bear the most burden of war. Armed conflicts often disrupt family and community networks, and thus raise the overall workload for women as they are forced to assume new roles. They take on triple, sometimes quadruple roles; family breadwinner, household leadership (entirely new to some women as men usually take charge of these roles), caregiver as well as creating public networks with other women (see Fig. 2.2). The gender-related impact of conflict on family demography leads to increased widow and female-headed households (FHH) in post-conflict settings. Changes in gender roles have the largest impact on women as caregivers, particularly when they become the head of a household, the breadwinner, and decision–maker. The participation of women in the labour market increases during and after conflict. Furthermore, women in post-conflict setting have organized themselves

Fig. 2.2 Woman, headed of household (HH), breadwinner and caregiver (This photo was taken by the research assistant Abd-Alrahman Ibrahim, 2016)

into social groups (in some cases political groups) to support each other and their community.

Goldstein (2001) states that armed conflict is constructed by gender. Consequently, the impacts of war to some extent are gendered. Armed conflict often disrupts social roles and relations that are shaped by gender. Gender-related changes include increased female–to–male ratios, FHH, for instance, in post-conflict Rwanda, females comprise more than 60% of the population, and the majority of households are female-headed (Zuckerman and Greenberg 2004). Schindler (2010), who used the household survey data from post-war Rwanda, found the sex ratios (the number of males for every 100 females) were severely unbalanced and a high proportion of FHH in post-war Rwanda. Across Rwanda based on a demographic survey conducted by her government in 1996, women headed approximately 34% of all households—up from 21% prior to the violence. These numbers reflect a demographic imbalance (Berry 2015). However, Newbury and Baldwin (2001) argued that 34% properly underestimates the actual number because of the reluctance on the part of those surveyed to claim the status. Bouta et al. (2005) found that in Angola, Mozambique, and Somalia, widows represent more than 50% of all adult women-headed household. Buchanan-Smith and Jaspars (2007) indicate there has been a sharp rise in the number of FHH in Darfur, with some communities estimating that up to three-quarters of households are now female-headed, especially in IDP camps. War has caused profound demographic changes, with FHH reaching as high as 70% in war-affected areas of South Sudan (Guvele et al. 2003: 10). Brück and Schindler (2008) refers to FHH in post-war settings, as reaching up to 30% and more of the total number of households. More women in the post-armed conflict situation have been found to participate in paid work and perform more economic activities. As pointed by Arostegui (2013), the roles of women alter and expand during armed conflict as they participate in the struggles and take on more economic responsibilities and duties as heads of households. If women had not taken on these new roles, many would have risked their lives and well-being, as well as the lives and well-being of children under their care (Berry 2015). While Bouta and Frerks (2002) have identified seven major roles of women before, during, and after armed conflict, which include (a) women as victims of sexual abuse which is caused by the general breakdown in law and order and a policy to demoralize the enemy, (b) women as combatants who directly and indirectly participate in the armed conflict by being fighters and supporting their men in the war, (c) women for peace in the non-governmental sectors who work for resisting conflict itself, (d) women in formal peace politics who participate in peace talks and sign agreements, (e) women as coping and surviving actors who adapt their existing roles and activities within the conflict environment, (f) women as household heads who take up roles in the absence of their men, and (g) women holding informal/formal jobs during the time of conflict.

The transformation of gender roles and relations in multiple and dynamic ways—that sometimes leave enduring legacies in the post-war period, which can empower or marginalize women (Wood 2008). War can serve as a period of rapid social change that can trigger a reconfiguration of gender roles by precipitating three interrelated and overlapping shifts: a demographic shift, an economic shift, and a cultural shift (Berry 2018).

There is a plethora of evidence indicating that intra-household gendered division of labour is similar in African patriarchal societies; it is culturally determined that women occupy roles such as care work and the household arrangements (see for example, Ibnouf and Ibnouf 2016 [Sudan]; Lusiba 2017 [Uganda]; Robles 2012 [Ethiopia and Tanzania]; Sikod 2007 [Cameroon]). Nonetheless, it is well known that conflict has often challenged traditional gender division of labour. This challenge favours women (see for example, Arostegui 2013; Luna et al. 2017). Consequently, the gains from years of conflict for women have been a positive shift in their roles. They assume new independent or increased roles as decision-making in households and in their communities formerly performed by men. Women become breadwinners of the family, meaning more laborious responsibilities to ensure provision of essential needs of their families. Thus, they become major active members of the labour market. Exiting literature shows an increase in the participation of women in the labour force, mostly informal, during and at the end of the conflict in Sudan, Angola, Mali, Uganda, and Somalia (El-Bushra and Sahl 2005). Manchanda (2005) points out that the feminization of the informal sector is a phenomenon of post-conflict societies. In such a situation, many families have been left without their primary breadwinners, menfolk. Due to the absence of men, women engage in activities previously considered "men's work" such as the construction of housing and ownership and management of their own businesses as petty traders or vendors of farm and forest products in the local markets, and even engage in informal activities, to mention but a few. This can be attributed to the fact that wars removed social barriers and change traditional patriarchal patterns. Thus women take on more "men's work" which shifts conventional social expectations for them. These changing roles due to the absence of men contribute to improving the skills of women, strengthening their independence and confidence and also changing the traditional domination of men on household's decision–making. El-Bushra's (2003) field research carried out in Sudan, Somalia, Uganda, Mali, and Angola concluded that conflict has undoubtedly given women greater responsibilities and with them the possibility of exerting greater leverage in decision-making and increasing their political participation. Nakamura (2004) points out that conflict has the potential of increasing the bargaining and decision-making power of women within households due to their increased socio-economic contribution to household income. Women's gains after war are often short-lived, as international actors, domestic political structures, and revitalized patriarchal norms combine to undermine their progress (Berry 2018).

Kabeer (2001: 19) states, "empowerment refers to the expansion in people's ability to make life choices in a context where this ability was previously denied". That is, it implies a process of change. In wartime as in its aftermath, the role of women increasingly change from housewife to household head, breadwinner, household decision-maker, and activist in peacebuilding. Consequently, some scholars argue that the empowerment of women is often a positive product of war. Thus, peacebuilding and post-conflict reconstruction could create a window of opportunity for the empowerment of women and potentially result in a post-conflict society with increased gender equality (Smet 2009). The post-conflict setting can be seen as a window of opportunity to challenge gender stereotypes: empower women, establish new gender norms, and possibly enhance women's positions in a post-conflict society (Zuckerman and Greenberg 2004). But the reality is different in the aftermath of conflict as these gains may be temporary due to the patriarchal attitudes of the society which remain unchanged. Several post-conflict experiences have demonstrated that the "gains" for women in terms of new gender roles are "lost" in the post-conflict period, when "going back to normal" is the priority—or when men are back from war. Schindler (2010) mentions studies cautioning that gender roles are only temporarily modified for the duration of the conflict and often return to the pre-conflict norm when the conflict ends. Nakamura (2004) confirms this by indicating that changes in gender roles, however, do not tend to be sustained after conflicts, instead pre-existing patriarchal gender roles re-emerge in post-conflict societies. Efforts to structurally change women's roles have been made with positive, but limited results in some conflict-affected countries. For instance, in Rwanda, there is an enhancement of women's political representation and participation in the national parliament, with women having won 56% of parliamentary seats in the 2008 elections, making it the place with the highest representation of women in the world (Sjoberg 2010: 171). The new constitutions in Uganda, Burundi, and the DRC adopted affirmative action mechanisms, especially quotas and cooptation systems, to help empower women economically and politically (Buvinic et al. 2013). Côte d'Ivoire represents a model of exclusion of women. The peace process here consists of a series of failed peace agreements and broken promises regarding elections (Hudson 2009: 289). Peace processes in South Sudan continue to exclude women from peacebuilding strategic plans (Adeogun and Muthuki 2018).

During the wartime, some people use the most brutal methods to defeat their enemy. In some violent conflict situations, there are no rules, no rights, no consideration and no respect, just total anarchy. Consequently, women and girls become the individual and group targets of sexual violence, specifically when rape and sexual assault are used as weapons of war or as one of the strategies of the conflict. Akinsulure-Smith (2014: 678) registers that scholars have documented the worldwide use of sexual violence against women throughout the ages and across cultures, calling it a weapon, strategy, instrument, and tool. Sexual violence, including the mass rape of women, has been highlighted as a widespread and systematic tool used in ethnic conflicts in many African countries including Rwanda, Uganda, and Darfur (Linos 2009). However, studies by Wood in 2006 and 2009 indicate that in most cases, sexual and gender-based violence is a crime of opportunity that is often committed by relatives rather than strangers (cited in Buvinic et al. 2013). In post-conflict domestic violence seems to be one of the decisive factors that contribute to the rollback of women's wartime gains and to the return to pre-war gender roles (Brück and Vothknecht 2011: 86). The repercussions of sexual violence for women are far-reaching and long-lasting at an individual level. Psychosocial consequences can include stigmatization and community rejection. When pregnant or with child, women can face further difficulties at a community. They can also be at risk of self-induced or enforced isolation (Anderson and Van Ee 2018). Haeri and Puechguirbal (2010) state that sexual violence continues to be an ugly component of many conflicts worldwide notwithstanding its explicit prohibition in international humanitarian law. Most rape cases during wartime are not reported to the concerned authorities for the fear of stigmatization. The common thread between all wars is that rape is a product of warped (yet normalized) militarized hegemonic masculinity, which arguably is structurally embedded in pre-conflict gender inequality and unequal power relations (Henry 2016). However, rape and sexual assault affects daily lives of women, rendering their caregiving activities during wartime onus.

Women have been involved in the fighting as combatants; nonetheless, their numbers have been rising steadily during recent years. Women have been actively involved as fighters in African countries such as

Angola, Eritrea, Ethiopia, Liberia, Mozambique, Sierra-Leone, South Africa, Uganda, and Zimbabwe (Coulter et al. 2008). The reason female combatants join an armed conflict might differ from that of the male combatants (Akbal 2017). In order to understand the reasons women engage in armed combat, it is crucial to understand the complexities of war, the society it is taking place in, the women's place within the respective society and the insurgent groups' sociology and ethics as well as its gender narrative (ibid.). Most female combatants may only engage in support roles as caregivers, while other women serve as combatants. As it has been argued by Wood (2008), civil war transforms traditional gender roles where patriarchal networks are often radically reshaped due to the involvement of female combatants. Women have been an important contingent of the South Sudan People's Liberation Army (SPLA) during the first and second Sudanese civil wars and estimates put women at between 10 and 30% of the fighting forces in the Sierra Leone conflict (Haeri and Puechguirbal 2010). The latter authors advocate that even as they dispel the notion of female helplessness by taking up arms, female combatants confront their own set of challenges, including the risk of sexual abuse or harassment. Shekhawat (2015) writes that female fighters made up at least 25–30% of the total strength of the Eritrean People's Liberation Front. In general, female combatants challenged traditional gender norms of the patriarchal African society. Wood and Thomas (2017) link variations in women's roles in armed groups to differences in beliefs about gender hierarchies and gender-based divisions of labour inherent in the specific ideologies they adopt. Shekhawat (2015) argues that being female combatant introduces women to uniquely diverse experiences of empowerment and exploitation. However, Parpart (2017: 54) states that women joined the military in Zaire, yet most were poorly trained and consigned to traditional "feminine" roles. In Eritrea, the combatant women were limited to traditional feminine work. Thus, the gender division of labour in these militaries generally reinforced established gender hierarchies, despite official rhetoric (ibid.).

It may be difficult to develop a general conclusion regarding the impact of violent conflicts on women, as the experiences are many and diverse with specific cultural context in which the conflict takes place. But in general, women during and after violent armed conflict presume a multitude of different care work roles. Many cases show women's resilience and ability to cope and deal with challenges posed by violent armed conflicts. Changing gender roles during and after war means not only providing more caregiving services, but also taking on more responsibilities to improve the livelihood of their families by entering the labour market and undertaking roles in the community that are formerly occupied by men. Feminist and gender analysts have been recently calling for a thorough analysis of unpaid care work on women's time, health, their opportunities, and underlying assumptions of stereotyping roles, and the persistence of gender inequalities (Narayan 2017: 655).

Notes

1. Global Trends UNHCR (2017). www.unhcr.org/dach/wpcontent/uploads/sites/27/2017/06/GlobalTrends2016.pdf.
2. Internally displaced persons (IDPs) defined by the United Nations (1998) "Persons or groups of persons who have been forced to flee or to leave their homes or places of habitual residence as a result of, or in order to avoid, in particular, the effects of armed conflict, situations of generalized violence, violations of human rights or natural or human made disasters, and who have not crossed an internationally recognized state border".

Bibliography

Abdul-Jalil, M.A. 2008. Nomad-Sedentary Relations and the Question of Land Rights in Darfur: From Complementarity to Armed Conflict. In *Nomadic-Sedentary Relations and Failing State Institutions in Darfur and Kordofan (Sudan)*, ed. R. Rottenburg, 1–24. Halle, Germany: Halle-Wittenberg University.

Adeogun, T.J., and J.M. Muthuki. 2018. Feminist Perspectives on Peacebuilding: The Case of Women's Organizations in South Sudan. *Agenda* 32 (2): 1–10.

Adisa, R.S., and O.A. Adekunle. 2010. Farmer-Herdsmen Conflicts: A Factor Analysis of Socio-economic Conflict Variables Among Arable Crop Farmers in North Central Nigeria. *Journal of Human Ecology* 30 (1): 1–9.

Ajibo, H. 2018. Dynamics of Farmers and Herdsmen Conflict in Nigeria: The Implication for Social Work Policy Intervention. *International Journal of Humanities and Social Science* 8 (7): 156–163. Published Online July 2018. https://doi.org/10.30845/ijhss.v8n7p16.

Akbal, G.P. 2017. Female Combatants: Same Goals, Different Motivations? E-International Relations Studies. https://www.e-ir.info.

Akinboade, O.A. 2005. A Review of Women, Poverty and Informal Trade Issues in East and Southern Africa. *International Social Science Journal* 57 (184): 255–275.

Akinsulure-Smith, A.M. 2014. Displaced African Female Survivors of Conflict-Related Sexual Violence: Challenges for Mental Health Providers. *Violence Against Women* 20 (6): 677–694.

Ali, H.E. 2014. *Darfur's Political Economy: A Quest for Development*, 1st ed. London: Routledge and Taylor & Francis Ltd.

Anderson, K., and E. Van Ee. 2018. Mothers with Children Born of Sexual Violence: Perceptions of Global Experts Regarding Support in Social Care Settings. *Health Care for Women International* 27: 1–19. Published Online 27 December 2018. https://doi.org/10.1080/07399332.2018.1522319.

Aremu, J.O. 2010. Conflicts in Africa: Meaning, Causes, Impact and Solution. *African Research Review* 4 (4), 17: 549–560. Published Online 17 October 2010. http://dx.doi.org/10.4314/afrrev.v4i4.69251.

Arostegui, J. 2013. Gender, Armed Conflict, and Peace-Building: How Armed Conflict Can Catalyze Positive Change for Women. *Gender & Development* 21 (3): 533–549. Published Online 11 November 2013. http://dx.doi.org/10.1080/13552074.2013.846624.

Berry, M.E. 2015. From Violence to Mobilization: Women, War, and Threat in Rwanda. *Mobilization: An International Quarterly* 20 (2): 135–156.

Berry, M.E. 2018. *From Violence to Mobilization: War, Women, and Political Power in Rwanda and Bosnia-Herzegovina*. New York: Cambridge University Press.

Bouta, T., and G. Frerks. 2002. *Women's Roles in Conflict Prevention, Conflict Resolution and Post-conflict Reconstruction: Literature Review and Institutional Analysis*. The Hague: Clingendael Institute.

Bouta, T., G. Frerks, and I. Bannon. 2005. *Gender, Conflict, and Development*. Washington, DC: World Bank.

Brück, T., and K. Schindler. 2008. The Impact of Conflict and Fragility on Households a Conceptual Framework with Reference to Widows. Research Paper No. 2008/83, UNU World Institute for Development Economics Research (UNU-WIDER).

Brück, T., and M. Vothknecht. 2011. Impact of Violent Conflicts on Women's Economic Opportunities. In *Women and War: Power and Protection in the 21st Century*, ed. K. Kuehnast, C. de Jonge Oudraat, and H. Hernes, 85–114. Washington, DC: United States Institute of Peace Press.

Buchanan-Smith, M., and S. Jaspars. 2007. Armed Conflict, Camps and Coercion: The Ongoing Livelihoods Crisis in Darfur. *Disasters* 31 (s1): 57–76.

Buvinic, M., M. Das Gupta, U. Casabonne, and P. Verwimp. 2013. Violent Conflict and Gender Inequality: An Overview. Policy Research Working Paper 6371, World Bank, Washington, DC.

Chynoweth, S.K., J. Freccero, and H. Touquet. 2017. Sexual Violence Against Men and Boys in Conflict and Forced Displacement: Implications for the Health Sector. *Reproductive Health Matters* 25 (51): 1–5. Published Online 11 December 2017. https://doi.org/10.1080/09688080.2017.1401895.

Cohen, D.K., A.H. Green, and E.J. Wood. 2013. Wartime Sexual Violence: Misconceptions, Implications, and Ways Forward. USIP Special Report 323, United States Institute of Peace, Washington, DC. https://www.usip.org/sites/default/files/resources/SR323.pdf.

Coulter, C., M. Persson, and M. Utas. 2008. *Young Female Fighters in African Wars: Conflict and Its Consequences*. Uppsala: Nordic Africa Institute.

El-Bushra, J. 2003. Fused in Combat: Gender Relations and Armed Conflict. *Development in Practice* 13 (2–3): 252–265.

El-Bushra, J.I., and M.G. Sahl. 2005. Cycles of Violence: Gender Relations and Armed Conflict. Printed for ACORD—Agency for Co-operation and Research in Development (ACORD) by Ramco Printing Works, Nairobi, Kenya.

Elbadawi, I., and N. Sambanis. 2000. Why Are There So Many Civil Wars in Africa? Understanding and Preventing Violent Conflict. *Journal of African Economies* 9 (3): 244–269.

Eweka, O., and T.O. Olusegun. 2016. Management of Internally Displaced Persons in Africa: Comparing Nigeria and Cameroon. *Africa Research Review: An International Multidisciplinary Journal* 10 (1): 193–210. Published Online January 2016. http://dx.doi.org/10.4314/afrrev.v10i1.15.

Ferris, E.G. 2007. Abuse of Power: Sexual Exploitation of Refugee Women and Girls. *Signs: Journal of Women in Culture & Society* 32 (3): 584–591.

Ferris, E. 2012. *Internal Displacement in Africa: An Overview of Trends and Opportunities*, 1–12. New York: Brookings-LSE Project on Internal Displacement.

Gates, S., H. Hegre, H.M. Nygård, and H. Strand. 2012. Development Consequences of Armed Conflict. *World Development* 40 (9): 1713–1722.

Ghobarah, H.A., P. Huth, and B. Russett. 2004. The Post-war Public Health Effects of Civil Conflict. *Social Science & Medicine* 59: 869–884.

Goldstein, J. 2001. *War and Gender: How War Shapes the Gender and Vice Versa*. Cambridge: Cambridge University Press.

Guvele, C., L.B. Deng, A. Itto, and B. D'Silva. 2003. Food Security Analysis. Institute of Development Studies (IDS), University of Sussex, Brighton. Analysis was presented at the Rumbek Strategy Meeting.

Haeri, M., and N. Puechguirbal. 2010. From Helplessness to Agency: Examining the Plurality of Women's Experiences in Armed Conflict. *International Review of the Red Cross* 92 (877): 103–122.

Henry, N. 2016. Theorizing Wartime Rape: Deconstructing Gender, Sexuality, and Violence. *Gender & Society* 30 (1): 44–56.

Hudson, H. 2009. Peacebuilding Through a Gender Lens and the Challenges of Implementation in Rwanda and Côte d'Ivoire. *Security Studies* 18 (2): 287–318.

Human Security Report. 2005. *War and Peace in the 21st Century: Assault on the Vulnerable*. University of British Columbia, Canada, Part III, 99–122. New York: Oxford University Press.

Ibnouf, M.A.O., and F.O. Ibnouf. 2016. Role of Rural Women in Sustaining Household Food Supplies in Western Sudan. *International Journal of Advanced Research* 4 (5): 455–469.

Jackson, R. 2002. Violent Internal Conflict and the African State: Towards a Framework of Analysis. *Journal of Contemporary African Studies* 20 (1): 29–52.

Kabeer, N. 2001. Reflections on the Measurement of Women's Empowerment. In *Discussing Women's Empowerment: Theory and Practice. SIDA Studies (3)*, ed. Anne Sisask, 17–57. Stockholm, Sweden: Swedish International Development Cooperation Agency.

Leander, A., and R. van Munster. 2007. Private Security Contractors in the Debate About Darfur: Reflecting and Reinforcing Neo-Liberal Governmentality. *International Relations* 21 (2): 201–216. Published Online June 2007. https://doi.org/10.1177/0047117807077004.

Linos, N. 2009. Rethinking Gender-Based Violence During War: Is Violence Against Civilian Men a Problem Worth Addressing? *Social Science and Medicine* 68 (8): 1548–1551.

Luna, K.C., G. Van Der Haar, and D. Hilhorst. 2017. Changing Gender Role: Women's Livelihoods, Conflict and Post-conflict Security in Nepal. *Journal of Asian Security and International Affairs* 4 (2): 175–195.

Lusiba, G.S. 2017. Intra-household Gender Division of Labor and Decision-Making on Rice Postharvest Handling Practices: A Case of Eastern Uganda. *Cogent Social Sciences* 3 (1): 1–14. Published Online 28 February 2017. https://doi.org/10.1080/23311886.2017.1296323.

Manchanda, R. 2005. Women's Agency in Peace Building: Gender Relations in Post-Conflict Reconstruction. *Economic and Political Weekly* 40 (44/45): 4737–4745.

Nakamura, F. 2004. *Gender and Armed Conflict in Africa: Challenges to Gender Roles, Relations and Identities in the Case of Mozambique*. Monterey, CA: Monterey Institute of International Studies.

Narayan, N. 2017. Contextualizing Unpaid Care Work and Women Empowerment. *International Journal of Applied Research* 3 (7): 654–659.

Nathan, L. 2006. No Ownership, No Peace: The Darfur Peace Agreement. Working Paper, No. 5 (Series 2), Crisis States Research Centre, London.

Newbury, C., and H. Baldwin. 2001. Profile: Rwanda—Civil War, Women and Gender Relations: Overview. In *Women and Civil War: Impact, Organizations, and Action*, ed. K. Kumar, 27–38. London and Boulder, CO: Lynne Rienner.

Parpart, J.L. 2017. Imagined Peace, Gender Relations and Post-conflict Transformation. In *Women, Gender Equality, and Post-conflict Transformation: Lessons Learned, Implication for the Future. Part One: Theory and Framework*, 2nd ed, ed. J.P. Kaufman and K.P. Williams, 51–72. London and New York: Routledge and Taylor & Francis Group.

Richards, J. 2014. Forced, Coerced and Voluntary Recruitment into Rebel and Militia Groups in the Democratic Republic of Congo. *The Journal of Modern African Studies* 52 (2): 301–326.

Robles, P.S. 2012. Gender Disparities in Africa's Labor Markets: An Analysis of Survey Datafrom Ethiopia and Tanzania. *Economies and Finances*. Université Paris-Est.

Schindler, K. 2010. Who Does What in a Household After Genocide?—Evidence from Rwanda. DIW Berlin Discussion Papers 1072, Berlin.

Shekhawat, S. 2015. Conflict, Peace and Patriarchy: Female Combatants in Africa and Elsewhere. *Conflict Trends* 4: 3–10.

Sideris, T. 2003. War, Gender and Culture: Mozambican Women Refugees. *Social Science and Medicine* 56: 713–724.

Sikod, Fo. 2007. Gender Division of Labour and Women's Decision-Making Power in Rural Households in Cameroon. *Africa Development* XXXII (3): 58–71. Council for the Development of Social Science Research in Africa (CODESRIA), Dakar.

Sjoberg, L. 2010. Reconstructing Women in Post-conflict Rwanda. In *Women, War, and Violence: Personal Perspectives and Global Activism*, ed. R.M. Chandler, L. Wang, and L.K. Fuller, 171–186. New York: Palgrave Macmillan.

Smet, S. 2009. A Window of Opportunity—Improving Gender Relations in Post-conflict Societies: The Sierra Leonean Experience. *Journal of Gender Studies* 18 (2): 147–163.

Tanner, V., and J. Tubiana. 2007. Divided They Fall: The Fragmentation of Darfur's Rebel Groups. HSBA Working Paper No. 6, Graduate Institute of International Studies, Geneva.

Thompson, M. 2006. Women, Gender, and Conflict: Making the Connections. *Development in Practice* 16 (3/4): 342–353.

Venkatasawmy, R. 2015. Ethnic Conflict in Africa: A Short Critical Discussion. *Transcience* 6 (2): 26–37.

Williams, P.D. 2008. Keeping the Peace in Africa: Why "African" Solutions Are Not Enough. *Carnegie Council for Ethics in International Affairs*: 309–329.

Wood, E.J. 2008. The Social Processes of Civil War: The Wartime Transformation of Social Networks. *Annual Review of Political Science* 11: 539–561. Published Online 4 March 2008. https://doi.org/10.1146/annurev.polisci.8.082103.104832.

Wood, R.M., and J.L. Thomas. 2017. Women on the Frontline: Rebel Group Ideology and Women's Participation in Violent Rebellion. *Journal of Peace Research* 54 (1): 31–46.

Zuckerman, E., and M. Greenberg. 2004. The Gender Dimensions of Post-conflict Reconstruction: An Analytical Framework for Policymakers. *Gender and Development* 12 (3): 70–82.

CHAPTER 3

Women and Unpaid Care Work: A Review

3.1 Initial Remarks

The literature on care work has now become ubiquitous. In recent years, the research on unpaid care work is viewed as a vital part of the global economy and women's economic empowerment. Three different sources of care are identified: the state, the family, and the market. Care work varies in meaning depending on the discipline: Sociology, health studies (disabilities, ageing, etc.), social policy, ethics, feminist scholarship, and other fields of study. Care is fundamental in shaping our individual identities as it defines the mannerisms through which we interact socially and build relationships. It is also primal in defining who we are and how we are viewed in both public and private spheres of life (Phillips 2007 cited in Reddy et al. 2014: 1). Esquivel (2013) states that "care is a crucial dimension of well-being and people need care throughout their lives in order to survive". Caregiving has been perceived as a feminine duty; it is a set of moral responses and practices; it can be paid or unpaid, and caregiving can be familial or communal. Various types of unpaid work have been identified, as (i) unpaid domestic work, (ii) unpaid subsistence activities, (iii) unpaid family work, (iv) unpaid work in paid workplaces, and (v) volunteering (Stuart 2014), each of which includes a subset of tasks. A substantial body of literature on unpaid care is continually invisible, unevaluated, unrecognized, and undervalued by society and policymakers. Caregiving usually volunteered by women goes unnoticed,

F. O. Ibnouf, *War-Time Care Work and Peacebuilding in Africa*, Gender, Development and Social Change,
https://doi.org/10.1007/978-3-030-26195-5_3

and is consistently undervalued or devalued in terms of material rewards and status (Zembylas et al. 2014). However, in recent years unpaid care work has generally been gaining importance in terms of recognition, and is being introduced into international development agendas. This is partly attributed to socio-economic, demographic, and political developments, increasingly making care a topic of interest among policymakers across developed and welfare states (Rummery and Fine 2012). Finally, there is an emerging consensus around its importance, based on an ever-growing body of evidence on the impact of unpaid care work on gender equality, women's rights and poverty (Woodroffe and Donald 2014). Notwithstanding the increasing volume of research devoted to this area of studies, many questions still remain unanswered. While much is understood about the burden of care work, and that women make up the most of caregivers, there is a rareness of information on the experiences of caregivers involved in the arrangement and provision of care in conflict or unfavourable circumstances.

3.2 Gender and Unpaid Care Work

There exists a vast amount of literature in sociology and social policy on gendered unpaid care work. Most feminist research puts forward the claim that women usually bore the brunt of unpaid care work. Women have been at the forefront of providing unpaid care (Dominelli 2002: 48). Duflo (2012: 1052) argues that women spend almost twice as much time on housework, around five times as much on child care, and about half as much time on market activities as men do. A review of published literature denotes that women and girls are the major care providers, yet the value of this work is rarely recognized (see for example, Corby et al. 2008). Hobbs and Rice (2018: 98) portray women as an essential source of unpaid work, due to the overarching belief that women possess natural capacities to efficiently carry out voluntary tasks. While care work remains a significant and unsupported activity, the likelihood of developing shared responsibilities may be remote (Rubery 2015). The male breadwinner versus female caregiver's polar representation perpetuates a gendering ideology that distorts and limits human potential and narrows the range of experiences of "being" and "doing" for men and women (Antonopoulos 2008).

Tavero et al. (2018) emphasizes three aspects of care; social invisibility, the relationship between care and gender roles, and its importance to the maintenance of life. It is a difficult situation between cultural expectations and society's needs. Women have continued to encounter discriminatory practices as a result of culturally derived expectations, such as solely bearing the responsibilities of unpaid care work. A number of studies from different parts of Africa affirm that women and men experience different socio-economic contexts and gender roles based on cultural expectations, which result in women being more likely to perform unpaid care work more likely than men (see for example, Berry 2018). The social ascription of care work to women can undermine their rights and limit their opportunities of self-development. Child upbringing and housekeeping are gender-biased activities ascribed to women which all came about as a result of socio-cultural socialization (Sikod 2007: 60). Across all regions of the world, women spend on average between three and six hours on unpaid care activities, while men spend between half an hour and two hours (Ferrant et al. 2014). Global statistics show that women spend at least twice as much time on unpaid domestic work as men, and the disparity is much greater in many developing countries (United Nations 2010). Around the world, women perform three times more unpaid care duties than men (UNDP 2015). Although women are now involved in activities previously dominated by men such as being a substantial part of the workforce, gaining higher education, etc., men have not reciprocally embraced activities usually carried out by women such as housework and childcare (Yavorsky et al. 2015).

Women are more responsible for care arrangements and are usually the main care providers in a humanitarian crises situation. In such situations, there is an increase in the demand for care in terms of quality and quantity and they generally assume primary care responsibilities for their family members in need of intensive care, especially those infected with HIV/AIDS (Corby et al. 2008). Furthermore, women and girls are also subsequently denied the supportive environment necessary to adhere to treatment and access to publicly funded care support services necessary for disease prevention and treatment (ibid.). Thus, caregiving which normally is supposed to be performed in the hospital by trained personnel is executed at the household level by untrained, unsupported, and unpaid women. In this case, the caregivers are vulnerable to contracting HIV/AIDS, as they are required to care for the sick. HIV/AIDS is recognized by Security Council Resolution 1308 of the United Nations Security Council as genuinely a threat to international peace and security (Rushton 2010). When addressing the HIV/AIDS crisis in African countries, Mindry (2010) states that humanitarian interventions should avoid invoking universal concepts of need but instead, it should draw on feminist ethics of intervention which emphasizes the efforts to balance rights, justice, and care in ways that take into account the web of relationships and the politics that shapes the realities of people in different contexts.

Some key aspects emerge from the literature on paid and unpaid gendered care work division of labour. Unpaid work responsibilities result in a gender gap in paid work (Elson 2017). According to Blackden and Wodon (2006), gender-biased division of labour, in which men are engaged in economic activities and women in domestic activities, is especially significant in Africa. Interventions designed to support women to participate in paid work are often based on assumptions around the elasticity of women's time (Maestre and Thorpe 2016). They fail to disaggregate household roles and responsibilities or to recognize care responsibilities outside the paid economy (ibid.). Unpaid work is linked with the location individuals occupy in paid work through many channels, such as it shapes the ability, duration, and types of paid work that can be undertaken and therefore limits access to existing and potential collective action processes and social security (Antonopoulos 2008). Gender remains significant in the division of both unpaid care work as time-use surveys have repeatedly shown, as well as in the structuring of the paid care economy (Razavi 2007). However, the literature on men as unpaid caregivers is still relatively sparse in Africa.

3.3 Unpaid Care Work in International Statements and Agreements

Literature holds that it was not until the 1970s that the introduction of 'women's issues as global issues' attracted widespread international attention and awareness (Shulika and Shulika 2016). The debate on domestic labour in the 1970s still makes important contributions to the current framing of unpaid care work. It questions the normalization of gendered labour in which domestic labour is seen as the "natural" responsibility of women, and points to the ways in which it is socially constructed and (de)valued (Rao 2018: 739). As a result, the first formal global recognition of unpaid care and domestic work came up at the Fourth International Women's Conference, held in 1995 in Beijing (ibid.). The Beijing Platform for Action acknowledges women's valuable yet unpaid contributions to development, in particular. It calls on Governments "to develop a more comprehensive knowledge of work and employment through, inter alia, efforts to measure and better understand the type, extent and distribution of unremunerated work, particularly work in caring for dependents and unremunerated work done for family farms and businesses".[1] Despite its international recognition, unpaid care work is overlooked in most African states. It is still not involved in development practices nor is it reflected in the GDP and/or GNP, and in the economic statistics essential for policy making.

A substantial body of diverse literature grapples with how unpaid care work influences international peacebuilding discourse. Razavi (2012) denotes that care has emerged or is emerging, as a legitimate subject of public debate and policy on the agendas of some civil society actors, developing country governments and international organizations. Yet, care needs have not been uniformly considered to be a rather public than a domestic agenda (Razavi 2012). There is no universally agreed upon definition of "care" and there are many different views on what it is and how it can be measured and how its burden can be reduced. Care work has been described by Razavi (2007) as a category of work which includes activities carried out in the service of others, deemed crucial for human well-being and economic development. Thus care work has an important contribution to economic development and the social well-being of the society. Other debates hold that unpaid care work must be valued by society, financially supported by governments, and shared more equally between women and men. The Millennium Development Goals (MDGs) represent the closest thing to a global consensus on developmental priorities (Gates et al. 2012: 1713). Nevertheless, unpaid care work was not specifically mentioned in the MDGs; notwithstanding that most of these goals depend on the provision of care work. Recently, unpaid care work has become prominent in the discourse of United Nations agencies such as the UNDP, UN-Women, UNCDF, and other international organizations such as International Labour Organization—ILO. The UN and its agencies have recognized the importance of unpaid care work, and they also agree that women and girls shoulder most of the burden of unpaid care worldwide. The UNDP in partnership with UN Women and UNCDF have launched the Inclusive Economic Local Development Initiative, which is working with local development programs to unlock private finance for infrastructural projects that would benefit women and lift their disproportionate burden of unpaid work (UNDP). The Convention on the Elimination of all Forms of Discrimination against Women (CEDAW) has recognized women's disproportionate burden of care in General recommendation 21, "The responsibilities that women have to bear and raise children will affect their right to access education, employment and other activities related to their personal development. It also imposes inequitable burdens of work on women". CEDAW demands affirmative measures for the preferential promotion of women and active political and legal steps for gender equality. Sudan and Somalia are the two African countries which have not hitherto ratified the Convention. Such affirmative measures have never been set into motion. Most of these international organizations such as the ILO have called for sweeping changes in policies which should address the rising need for care and tackle the huge disparity between female and male care responsibilities. These examples illustrate the enormous progress made in getting unpaid care work onto the international development agenda as a public policy issue. Yet in almost every case, since most caregivers are women, care is perceived to be a woman's duty (Esquivel 2014).

The 2030 Sustainable Development Goals (SDGs–Goal 5) has unequivocally highlighted the inclusion of "Unpaid Care Work and Domestic Work" as a target (target 5.4) in the approved agenda is a defining moment in the recognition and valuation of unpaid work (Narayan 2017: 654). The target states: "Recognize and value unpaid care and domestic work through the provision of public services, infrastructure and social protection policies and the promotion of shared responsibility within the household and the family as nationally appropriate" (ibid.). This formulation may not be perfect; still, just its presence is the result of almost half a century of debate, discussion, mobilization, and advocacy by feminist academics and activists around issues of domestic work, care work, the care economy, social reproduction, and unpaid/unremunerated work (Rao 2018: 736). Furthermore, there is little direction about how the SDGs 5.4 target is going to be achieved, policy and programs to be implemented, etc. At the regional level, the "Africa Agenda 2063" commits to the global agenda by fostering the development of joint programs that promote debates on women empowerment, and to continuously orient policy and decision makers to understand the important role that women play in development, and specifically in care (among others), by putting in place mechanisms for the empowerment of women (AU 2015).[2] International agreements and conventions, such as the SDGs, have the potential to make care visible at both national and international levels. However, challenges remain in terms of the implementation and the provision of quality and quantity of services needed. Nevertheless, most of the national policies are quiet on program specifics to address unpaid care work or how to lessen its burden on women, particularly in African countries.

3.4 Valuing Unpaid Care Work—Valuing Women as Caregivers

Because unpaid care work is unevenly distributed between women and men, it is important to understand its magnitude, dynamics, and impact (Fälth and Blackden 2009). How has the state actually calculated the contribution of women's unpaid work to its development at normal times, talk less of during wartime? Some scholars have articulated unpaid care work as not considered to be socially, economically, and politically job. The valuation of unpaid work is still statistically imperceptible in most African countries, let alone wartime care work. There is little or no survey information on periodic care activities carried out by men and women, and on how much time each spend in fulfilling these activities. In developing countries, most studies on unpaid work effectuated by women focuses on the production of tangible goods (e.g. subsistence farming) while ignoring the production of intangible goods (e.g. care work) (Budlender 2010).

Unpaid care work has important implications for well-being and gender equality. It has been regarded as significant beyond the scope of economic and social policies and contributes to the market economy by maintaining a healthy, productive workforce (Rost 2018), though it is generally not classified as being productive work and ignored in the national statistical accounts. This can be attributed to the fact that existing standards' measurement and records are jobs only. For example, household child care is not accounted for in the GNP. However, it is as if the caregiver earns wages, such as a nursery school or kindergarten staff. Valuing unpaid care work can be resolved by adopting the specialized market replacement method. Here, the number of hours spent in unpaid care work is multiplied by the wage equal to that of job owners engaged in paid care work. Unpaid care work is increasingly being included in policy making and is elaborated by different international agencies and policymakers (Maestre and Thorpe 2016) point out that care is work because it has costs—both time and energy. Similar to (Elson 2000) insists that it is work because it is an activity that has costs in terms of time and energy. The UN Fourth World Conference on Women in Beijing (1995) has recommended the valuation of women's unpaid work and its inclusion in conventional estimates of national input.[3] There are existing methods for measuring the economic and monetary value of unpaid work. Nonetheless, valuing unpaid work is particularly difficult in wartime, as it is associated with grief and frustration for the affected. One of the most unique methods of collecting data on these economic activities in the non-market sector is time-use surveys (Stuart 2014). It is also possible to put a monetary value on unpaid work by evaluating the cost of hiring someone to do the work instead (Elson 2017). Oxfam's Women's Economic Empowerment and Care (WE-Care) program has developed a Household Care Survey (HCS) to capture different aspects of care work (Rost 2018). HCS takes an innovative approach to measuring care work that accounts for care activities carried out simultaneously (ibid.).

Besides the contribution of unpaid care work to human and social capital formation, it also plays a pivotal role in generating and sustaining economic growth (Folbre and Nelson 2000). Leonard (2003: 82) states that:

> A gender perspective is adopted in development that means widening the definitions of work to incorporate the various roles that women perform, and also recognizing women as active economic agents, particularly in the informal and household sectors of the economy.

It has also been argued that care is an intrinsic goal of development, as it is essential for maintaining human reproduction and life (Folbre 2006). While women have been disempowered by their traditional specialization in care work, both within and without the family provides important resources for the development of human capabilities (Folbre 2006). Care work contributes to well-being, social development, and economic growth, but the costs of providing care are unequally borne across gender and social class (Razavi and Silke 2012). Care work has a market value, but since the home is not generally regarded as a workplace—tasks performed inside the household for free are not regarded as being "real" work. Therefore, traditional measures of productivity like the Gross Domestic Product (GDP) does not record unpaid care work. But if included in the national accounts, the unpaid care economy would represent between 15 and over 50% of national GDP (Woodroffe and Donald 2014), the calculations vary because it depends on country and method (see Budlender 2010). The McKinsey Global Institute (MGI)[4] estimates that the total output of unpaid care work would be about $10 trillion, roughly 13% of global GDP, notwithstanding the efforts of Diane Elson (2000) who thinks that women's activities are often not "counted" in statistics, nor "accounted for" in representations of the economy, and not "taken into account" in policy making. The activities that do not involve monetary flows become invisible, and are neither seen nor valued and because care work is neither paid nor valued it is not measured; because it is not visible it is not taken into account in policymaking (Orozco 2009). Thus, it is not included in the national statistical accounts such as the GDP or the gross national product (GNP), which are usually used for policymaking. GDP and GNP focus only on market productive activities. Unpaid work would account for at least half of a given country's total GNP (ILO 2007 cited in Hobbs and Rice 2018: 97).

Women and girls as caregivers are not included in neither work-force surveys nor the value of their work in GDP statistics. Thus their efforts are not represented in the data informing policy making (Narayan 2017: 656). Recommendations from surveys emphasize the contribution of care provision to economic development. Countries need to recognize care work as a valuable and skilled activity that needs to be invested in. Recognizing unpaid care and domestic work means understanding how this work underpins all economies and valuing it accordingly (Elson 2017). The provision of care is a social good and valuable activity that is essential for maintaining the society (Maestre and Thorpe 2016). The fulfilment of care responsibilities represents an indispensable contribution to the maintenance of social capital (Folbre 2006). Valuing unpaid care in national accounts means it can be used in designing economic and social policies. A number of studies have come to the same conclusion. The amount of unpaid care work carried out and the way the burden of this work is distributed across different individuals have important implications for the well-being of individuals and households, as well as for economic dynamism and growth (Budlender 2010). Unpaid care work is a critical dimension of human well-being that provides essential domestic services within the household (Fälth and Blackden 2009). Gender advocates have put forward a range of proposals that attempt to overcome the many disadvantages endured by most women because of their responsibilities as caregivers (Razavi 2007). The provision of care may be stylishly conceptualized as a "care diamond" to include the family/household, markets, the public sector, and the not-for-profit sector (ibid.). Women as caregivers during and in the aftermath of war live in critical and stressful conditions. In such times of hardship, women expand their role to involve all types of life-saving care work. Exposing unpaid care work and its inclusion in national agendas will contribute to achieving economic empowerment of women, promote gender equality, family and societal well-being, and sustain peace in a much broader sense. The failure to socialize the costs of care will feed into and exacerbate existing gender inequalities (Razavi 2012).

3.5 Care Work in Armed Conflict—The Missing Link

Much has been written about the roles and status of women during wartime in Africa. Most of the literature on conflicts and wars still perceive women primarily as armed conflict powerless victims (see for example, Coulter et al. 2008). To date the impact of conflict, women has focused almost entirely on sexual and gender-based violence (Buvinic et al. 2013). Though the roles of women during and in the aftermath of war vary widely, they are still expected to bear the brunt of unpaid care work and household chores by meeting up with the growing needs essential for the survival of their families. Time and time again, women are labelled victims and put in the category of vulnerable people together with children, irrespective of the increasing responsibilities they take over in the absence of men (Puechguirbal 2012: 5). Care work during wartime and aftermath is expressly referred to only in a limited manner and has not been given special attention in peacebuilding discourse and conflict transformation studies. The literature on conflict studies distinguishes the direct effects of conflicts (killing, wounding, and physical destruction that result from violence), from the indirect effects as on economic performance and human welfare (Buvinic et al. 2013). Death and destruction alter the structure and dynamics of households, including their demographic profiles and traditional gender roles. The post-conflict situation is associated with the demographic transition where the absence of men (as legitimate targets, as members of armed forces or as rebel groups) has magnified the role of women in care work. The demand for caregiving increases and magnifies due to the various negative consequences associated with the war. Thus, women as caregivers have to struggle desperately to make ends meet.

There has been an emergent body of literature from diverse disciplines converging around questions of care (Razavi 2007), including anthropology, sociology, human rights, gender and women studies, healthcare work. According to Rao (2018: 738) discussions around unpaid care and domestic work emerged in the late 1960s and early 1970s in what has been called the "domestic-labour debate". The literature on women during conflict largely neglects the ways in which women might be affected by war. It focuses on sexual violence and ignores the agency of women (Akbal 2017). The agency of women is socio-culturally determined and their experiences vary across space and time (ibid.). Humanitarian discourses continue to portray women as victims and end up devaluing the multiple (empowering) roles women take on during conflict in managing community survival and peacebuilding (Manchanda 2005). Feminists have argued that women's daily experiences and struggles enable them to articulate different perspectives on peacebuilding that challenges dominant male discourse on conflict and peacebuilding (Adeogun and Muthuki 2018). Black and African feminist scholars have further called for openness to the multiplicity and diversity of women's experiences, including in situations of conflict and post-conflict (ibid.). Making the variety of women's experiences visible and documented allows us to stop taking men's experiences and privileges for granted (Puechguirbal 2012: 5). Thompson (2006) states:

> Practice has shown that if we don't understand the specific circumstances, experiences, roles, vulnerabilities, and capacities of men and women in war, we construct homogeneous strategies of response that do not address gender-based differences and generally tend to put women at a disadvantage.

Conversely Haeri and Puechguirbal (2010) argue for the need to consider the plurality of women's experiences in war, including as female heads of households, as victims (and survivors) of sexual violence, as community leaders, and as armed combatants. The inclusion of African women in peace processes will ensure that a wide range of experiences, perspectives, and faculty can be brought to bear in peace processes (Iwilade 2011: 35).

In the armed conflict studies literature, care work is mentioned here and there when dealing with topics such as armed conflict and health, women's role in the post-armed conflict, etc. In broad terms, it is said that armed conflict situations have negative impacts on health (that is, care needs are increased) and diminish the state's ability to provide care. Siem (2017) thinks in times of conflict, the number of persons in need of emergency medical care increases substantially, people are wounded in attacks, while deterioration in living conditions increases the number of the sick. As a consequence, civil society, and particularly women in civil society, is overloaded with care work. The increase in care needs is determined by the negative Impact of conflict on health (e.g. increased disability). WHO (2011) report recognizes that "armed conflict generates injuries and trauma that can result in disabilities". It has been argued that armed conflict directly affects all the major contributors to health: exposure to disease, medical care, public health interventions, and overall socio-economic conditions (Ghobarah et al. 2004: 871). For those incurring such injuries, the situation is often exacerbated by delays in obtaining emergency health care and longer-term rehabilitation. Gates et al. (2012: 1715) argues that the inability or unwillingness of states to provide health services for their population during wartime, or in refugee camps, increase the transmission of diseases. Relatively little is known about care arrangements in armed conflict and post-armed conflict situations or about how violent armed conflict affects the care arrangement as a whole. Without adequate recognition and support, unpaid care work can undermine women's human rights and dignity. The unpaid care work women arrangement in wartime and aftermath is indispensable and very essential for urgent survival needs and well-being of their family and community. Less attention to wartime caregiving can be traced back to that care work often regarded as woman's routine activity.

There has not been much exploration on the impact of conflict on access to maternal health care services. The literature on this issue is reduced to maternal mortality in armed conflict areas. Several ethnographic and qualitative studies have noted a link between conflict and utilization of maternal health care. These studies suggest that violent conflict reduces health care utilization through the destruction of health care facilities, intimidation of medical personnel, and by creating an atmosphere of insecurity that discourages travel (Price and Bohara 2013). Armed conflict poses serious challenges to access quality maternal and reproductive health services in Burundi and Northern Uganda, resulting in increased maternal morbidity and mortality (Chi et al. 2015). Maternal health care services are very limited and access to them unsecured. Thus, women in Darfur are more likely to die during pregnancy, delivery, and the postpartum period (Adam 2015).

3.6 The Absence of Women from Peacebuilding Processes

The essential role of women in peacebuilding is internationally recognized as can be seen in various policy documents. Over the recent decades, women and peacebuilding has been an emerging research field. However, the voices of women have been ignored in peace negotiations and talks, especially in Africa. Iwilade (2011: 32) points out African women still face tremendous challenges in effectively participating in peace talks. Between 1992 and 2011, just 2% of chief mediators and 9% of negotiators in peace processes were women.[5] Nonetheless, the security discourse and agenda have widened their scope since the 1990s to include new actors and topics, such as gender, equity, and the environment (Bain 1999).

Since the enactment of United Nations Security Council Resolution (UNSCR 1325), much lip service has been paid to women's critical role in peacebuilding, yet the reality is that women continue to be excluded from formal peace processes (Noma et al. 2012). Since the remarkable UNSCR 1325, women still remain significantly under-represented in peace and transitional processes (Paffenholz et al. 2016). The UNSCR 1325 (2000) is the first Security Council resolution to deal with the impact of armed conflicts on women and girls in all phases of peace processes, which has raised international awareness, as evidenced by these three follow-up resolutions—SCRs 1820, 1888, and 1889 (Rehn and Sirleaf 2009). Through the unanimous adoption of resolution 1889 (2009), the Council reaffirmed its landmark 2000 resolution 1325 on "Women, Peace and Security" (United Nations 2009). An examination of all peace processes after civil wars reveals that less than 10% of women are included, as envisioned in the UNSCR 1325 (Ellerby 2016). The main points of the UNSCRs (1325, 1820, 1888, and 1889) have been focused on the participation of women in conflict prevention and peace building and on the promotion and respect of women's rights in general. For instance, UNSCR 1325 (2000) focuses on the equal participation of women in all efforts for the maintenance and promotion of peace and security. The greater stress of the UNSCR 1820 (2008) stresses on prevention and punishment of sexual violence not the inclusion, yet women have managed to make substantial contributions to peace making and constitution-making negotiations, and to the eventual implementation of negotiated agreements (Paffenholz et al. 2016). The critical areas of concern to women and wartime care work have not been sufficiently addressed. There still is an insufficient appreciation of the role women play in sustaining their families during and in the aftermath of war. The drudgery women carry out during wartime is under-represented.

3.7 The Implementation of UNSCR 1325 Through National Action Plans (NAPs) by African States

The UNSCR 1325[6] is hailed as a road map to promote women's full engagement in peace negotiations, and in post-armed conflict reconstructions. It deals with human rights issues and most especially, handling the problem of women in armed conflict affected areas. Previous UN resolutions treated women as victims of war, in need of protection. However, UNSCR 1325 recognizes women as agents in building peace and guaranteeing security (Pratt and Richter-Devroe 2011). The UNSCRs 1820 and 1888 also have women specific clauses extolling women. Unfortunately, while attention is paid on issues of conflict-related sexual violence (UNSCRs 1820, 1888, and 1889), there is little attention to equally important issues of the impact of such violence on women as caregivers/providers during and after conflict. For example, in Uganda, NAP sensitized gender roles are somewhat avoided when the UNAP highlights masculinity and femininity/gender stereotypes, gender division of labour, and women's roles in the everyday (Hudson 2017).

A number of African countries have already developed National Action Plans (NAPs)[7] on the implementation of UNSCR 1325 Resolution, although it is still in the initial phase as for now. The launch of NAP is the first essential step towards enabling women's participation in the peacebuilding processes. According to Rehn and Sirleaf (2002), implementation and domestication of policy blueprints by member-states has been a challenge for many African states. 1325 asks that member-states should consider gender in peacebuilding processes. "Considering gender" requires more than acknowledging gender inequality and foregrounding women's needs in peace processes (Hudson 2009: 288). It also includes examining the impact of conflict on men and women and the unique knowledge and experiences that both groups bring to the peace table (ibid.). Ryan and Basini (2017: 201) studied NAPs in Liberia and Sierra Leone, and revealed that it refers to women more as victims than as actors and the prioritization of issues that reinforce rather than challenge gender role. Women's issues and needs are most likely to be resisted or subverted, because gendered power relations relegate these needs and issues to be personal or label them as "soft" issues (ibid.).

UNSCR 1325 is urging the various stakeholders to ensure that women have a part—and a say—in the peace process and in post-armed conflict reconstruction. In spite of the widespread support for the UNSCR 1325, most African countries affected by armed conflict, including in particular the Sudan, have not yet managed to implement it in a comprehensive and/or sustainable way even when some states have already launched a NAP. Planning processes that aim to translate international instruments into national policies are a challenge that requires sufficient funding, political will, and expertise, as well as building a broad-based consensus to work towards women's participation in peace and security issues and on the protection of their rights. However, the local ownership of the peace process is of course of monumental importance. It can help to ensure that peace is lasting. The UNSCR 1325 appears to be established on a significant body of feminist scholarship. It highlights the different experiences of war by men and women and redefines sexual violence as a weapon of war, rather than an "unfortunate by-product", and recognizes the significant role played by women at the grassroots level in rebuilding the lives of their communities after armed conflict (see Pratt and Richter-Devroe 2011).

Various measures have been employed in order to enforce the position of women in post-war countries, such as establishing a gender quota within governments or laws to counteract violence against women. But such measures do not count for much if they are not implemented. Despite the quota system in the parliament, women are represented numerically, but they do have a real impact on women in conflict areas. Rwanda leads the African continent in female parliamentary representation. Increased women's representation in Rwanda has had little effect on policy outputs (Devlin and Elgie 2008: 237). Throughout Africa, women are still sorely under-represented in political decision-making, which if it takes place, it will lead to a fair society. The peace agreement paved the way for a broad mobilization of Sudanese women, allowing for new issues to be adopted ranging from the adoption of 25% women's quota in the legislature, and many other concerns (Tønnessen and Al-Nagar 2013). Nonetheless, the reformation of some laws in Sudan have not yet achieved as much as criminalizing of FGM at the national level (ibid.).

It is not just about peace, but about peace and a just society that takes into consideration the needs and interests of women as they do those of men. It is about positive peace that provides for social justice and equity, plies prerogatives related to the roles of women, transforms gender relations in society, and that redefines gendered hierarchies (Sebhatu 2017). "Gender-neutral" rests on men's perspectives of war and peace. It overlooks women's needs as well as expectations in post-conflict. In addition, it illustrates how the negotiations for peace are maintained in the hands of the men who fought in the war and became the new peacemakers, even if they had violated the rights of women during the conflict (Puechguirbal 2012: 6). In Africa, there are examples (Somalia, Burundi, Rwanda, Sierra Leone, DRC, Mozambique, South Africa, Angola, etc.) of the activism of women for peace during conflicts (Shulika and Shulika 2016). Yet, women often remain side-lined and excluded from the negotiating tables and from high priority decision-making processes, especially during conflict and in the aftermath of conflict (ibid.). Care needs to be in the NAP agenda, policy, and programming design.

Notes

1. Paragraphs 68 (b) and 165 (g) of the Beijing Platform for Action—(2015), Beijing+20: Review of implementation of the Beijing Declaration and Platform for Action in the Arab region, National Reports. Available at http://www.escwa.un.org/sites/beijingplus20/documents.asp.
2. AU Declaration on 2015 Year of Women's Empowerment and Development Towards Africa's Agenda 2063. https://www.tralac.org/news/article/7611-au-declaration-on-2015-year-of-women-s-empowerment-and-development-towards-africa-s-agenda-2063.html.
3. Beijing Declaration and Platform for Action the UN Fourth World Conference on Women in Beijing. http://www.un.org/womenwatch/daw/beijing/pdf/BDPfA%20E.pdf.
4. In 2015, the McKinsey Global Institute published the power of parity: How advancing women's equality can add $12 trillion to global growth. McKinsey Global Institute. http://www.mckinsey.com/mgi/overview.
5. UN Women, "Women's Participation in Peace Negotiations: Connections between Presence and Influence", October 2012, p. 3.
6. The United Nations Security Council Resolution (UNSCR 1325) was adopted unanimously on 31 October 2000, after recalling resolutions 1261 (1999), 1265 (1999), 1296 (2000), and 1314 (2000).
7. African countries with NAPs include Côte d'Ivoire (2007), Uganda (2008), Liberia (2009), Guinea (2009), Sierra Leone (2010), Rwanda (2010), the Democratic Republic of the Congo (2010), Guinea-Bissau (2011), Burundi

(2011), Togo (2011), Senegal (2011), Mali (2012), Burkina Faso (2012), Ghana (2012), Nigeria (2013), Central African Republic (2014), Gambia (2014), Kenya (2016), and South Sudan (2016) (Hudson 2017).

References

Adam, I.F. 2015. The Influence of Maternal Health Education on the Place of Delivery in Conflict Settings of Darfur, Sudan. *Conflict & Health* 9 (1): 31. Published Online 5 October 2015. https://doi.org/10.1186/s13031-015-0057-2.

Adeogun, T.J., and J.M. Muthuki. 2018. Feminist Perspectives on Peacebuilding: The Case of Women's Organizations in South Sudan. *Agenda* 32 (2): 1–10.

Akbal, G.P. 2017. Female Combatants: Same Goals, Different Motivations? E–International Relations Studies. https://www.e-ir.info.

Antonopoulos, R. 2008. The Unpaid Care Work Paid Work Connection. Working Paper, No. 541, Levy Economics Institute of Bard College, Annandale-on-Hudson, NY.

Bain, W. 1999. Against Crusading: The Ethic of Human Security and Canadian Foreign Policy. *Canadian Foreign Policy Journal* 6 (3): 85–98.

Berry, M.E. 2018. *From Violence to Mobilization: War, Women, and Political Power in Rwanda and Bosnia-Herzegovina*. New York: Cambridge University Press.

Blackden, C.M., and Q. Wodon. 2006. Gender, Time Use, and Poverty in Sub-Saharan Africa. Working Paper 73, The World Bank, Washington, DC.

Budlender, D. 2010. *Time Use Studies and Unpaid Care Work*, 1st ed. New York: Routledge.

Buvinic, M., M. Das Gupta, U. Casabonne, and P. Verwimp. 2013. Violent Conflict and Gender Inequality: An Overview. Policy Research Working Paper 6371, World Bank, Washington, DC.

Chi, P.C., P. Bulage, H. Urdal, and J. Sundby. 2015. Perceptions of the Effects of Armed Conflict on Maternal and Reproductive Health Services and Outcomes in Burundi and Northern Uganda: A Qualitative Study. *BMC International Health and Human Rights* 15 (7): 1–15. Published Online 3 April 2015. https://doi.org/10.1186/s12914-015-0045-z.

Corby, N., N. O'Farrell, M. Podmore, and C. Sepulveda Zelaya. 2008. *Walking the Talk: Putting Women's Rights at the Heart of the HIV and AIDS Response*. London: ActionAid and Voluntary Services Overseas.

Coulter, C., M. Persson, and M. Utas. 2008. *Young Female Fighters in African Wars: Conflict and Its Consequences*. Uppsala: Nordic Africa Institute.

Devlin, C., and R. Elgie. 2008. The Effect of Increased Women's Representation in Parliament: The Case of Rwanda. *Parliamentary Affairs* 61 (2): 237–254. Published Online April 2008. https://doi.org/10.1093/pa/gsn007.

Dominelli, L. 2002. *Feminist Social Work Theory and Practice*. Basingstoke: Palgrave Macmillan.

Duflo, E. 2012. Women Empowerment and Economic Development. *Journal of Economic Literature* 50 (4): 1051–1079. Published Online December 2012. http://dx.doi.org/10.1257/jel.50.4.1051.

Ellerby, K. 2016. A Seat at the Table Is Not Enough: Understanding Women's Substantive Representation in Peace Processes. *Peacebuilding* 4 (2): 136–150.

Elson, D. 2000. *Progress of the World's Women 2000: UNIFEM Biennial Report*. New York: United Nations Development Fund for Women.

Elson, D. 2017. Recognize, Reduce, and Redistribute Unpaid Care Work: How to Close the Gender Gap. *New Labor Forum* 26 (2): 52–61.

Esquivel, V. 2013. Care in Households and Communities: Background Paper on Conceptual Issues, Oxfam Research Report. ISBN: 978-1-78077-473-2.

Esquivel, V. 2014. What Is a Transformative Approach to Care, and Why Do We Need It? *Gender & Development* 22 (3): 423–439.

Fälth, A., and M. Blackden. 2009. Unpaid Care Work. Gender Equality and Poverty Reduction Policy Brief, Issue 1, UNDP, New York.

Ferrant, G., L.M. Pesando, and K. Nowacka. 2014. Unpaid Care Work: The Missing Link in the Analysis of Gender Gaps in Labor Outcomes. Issue Paper, OECD Development Center.

Folbre, N. 2006. Measuring Care: Gender, Empowerment, and the Care Economy. *Journal of Human Development* 7 (2): 183–199. Published Online 22 January 2007. https://doi.org/10.1080/14649880600768512.

Folbre, N., and J.A. Nelson. 2000. For Love or Money—Or Both? *Journal of Economic Perspectives* 14 (4): 123–140.

Gates, S., H. Hegre, H.M. Nygård, and H. Strand. 2012. Development Consequences of Armed Conflict. *World Development* 40 (9): 1713–1722.

Ghobarah, H.A., P. Huth, and B. Russett. 2004. The Post-war Public Health Effects of Civil Conflict. *Social Science and Medicine* 59: 869–884.

Haeri, M., and N. Puechguirbal. 2010. From Helplessness to Agency: Examining the Plurality of Women's Experiences in Armed Conflict. *International Review of the Red Cross* 92 (877): 103–122.

Hobbs, M.H., and C. Rice. 2018. *Gender and Women's Studies: Critical Terrain*, 2nd ed. Canada: Women's Press.

Hudson, H. 2009. Peacebuilding Through a Gender Lens and the Challenges of Implementation in Rwanda and Côte d'Ivoire. *Security Studies* 18 (2): 287–318.

Hudson, H. 2017. The Power of Mixed Messages: Women, Peace, and Security Language in National Action Plans from Africa. *Africa Spectrum* 52 (3): 3–29.

Iwilade, A. 2011. Women and Peace Talks in Africa. *Journal of International Women's Studies* 12 (1): 22–37.

Leonard, M. 2003. Women and Development: Examining Gender Issues in Developing Countries. In *From the Local to the Global Key Issues in Development*

Studies, ed. G. McCann and S. McCloskey, 76–92. London and Sterling, Virginia: Pluto Press.

Maestre, M., and J. Thorpe. 2016. *Understanding Unpaid Care Work to Empower Women in Market Systems Approaches.* London: The BEAM Exchange.

Manchanda, R. 2005. Women's Agency in Peace Building: Gender Relations in Post-Conflict Reconstruction. *Economic and Political Weekly* 40 (44/45): 4737–4745.

Mindry, D. 2010. Engendering Care: HIV, Humanitarian Assistance in Africa, and the Reproduction of Gender Stereotypes. *Culture, Health and Sexuality* 12 (5): 555–568. Published Online 4 September 2014. https://doi.org/10.1080/13691051003768140.

Narayan, N. 2017. Contextualizing Unpaid Care Work and Women Empowerment. *International Journal of Applied Research* 3 (7): 654–659.

Noma, E., D. Aker, and J. Freeman. 2012. Heeding Women's Voices: Breaking Cycles of Conflict and Deepening the Concept of Peacebuilding. *Journal of Peacebuilding & Development* 7 (1): 7–32. Published Online 25 October 2012. https://doi.org/10.1080/15423166.2012.719384.

Orozco, A.P. 2009. Global Perspectives on the Social Organization of Care in Times of Crisis: Assessing the Situation. Working Paper 5: Gender, Migration and Development Series, United Nations International Research and Training, Institute for the Advancement of Women (INSTRAW).

Paffenholz, T., N. Ross, S. Dixon, A. Schluchter, and J. True. 2016. *Making Women Count—Not Just Counting Women: Assessing Women's Inclusion and Influence on Peace Negotiations.* Geneva: Inclusive Peace and Transition Initiative (The Graduate Institute of International and Development Studies) and UN Women.

Pratt, N., and S. Richter-Devroe. 2011. Critically Examining UNSCR 1325 on Women, Peace and Security. *International Feminist Journal of Politics* 13 (4): 489–503. Published Online December 2011. https://doi.org/10.1080/14616742.2011.611658.

Price, J.I., and A.K. Bohara. 2013. Maternal Health Care Amid Political Unrest: The Effect of Armed Conflict on Antenatal Care Utilization in Nepal. *Health Policy and Planning* 28 (3): 309–319. Published Online 6 December 2012. https://doi.org/10.1093/heapol/czs062.

Puechguirbal, N. 2012. The Cost of Ignoring Gender in Conflict and Post Conflict Situations: A Feminist Perspective. *Amsterdam Law Forum* 4 (1): 4–19. ISSN 1876-8156.

Rao, N. 2018. Global Agendas, Local Norms: Mobilizing Around Unpaid Care and Domestic Work in Asia. *Development and Change* 49 (3): 735–758.

Razavi, S. 2007. The Political and Social Economy of Care in a Development Context: Conceptual Issues, Research Questions and Policy Options. Gender and Development, Paper No. 3, UNRISD, Geneva.

Razavi, S. 2012. Rethinking Care in a Development Context: An Introduction. *Development and Change* 42 (4): 873–903.

Razavi, S., and S. Silke. 2012. Introduction: Care Workers in the Global Economy: Worlds Apart? In *Global Variations in the Political and Social Economy of Care*. New York: Routledge.
Reddy, V., S. Meyer, T. Shefer, and T. Meyiwa. 2014. Towards a Critical Theory of Care. In *Care in Context: Transnational Gender Perspectives*, ed. V. Reddy, S. Meyer, T. Shefer, and T. Meyiwa, 1–27. Cape Town: HSRC Press.
Rehn, E., and E.J. Sirleaf. 2002. *Women, War and Peace – Experts' Biographical Sketches*. United Nations Development Fund for Women (UNIFEM). https://www.unfpa.org/sites/default/files/pub-pdf/.
Rehn, E., and E.J. Sirleaf. 2009. Focus: Women, Gender and Armed Conflicts in ADC. *Gender Policy*. https://www.oecd.org/dac/gender-development/44896284.pdf.
Rost, L. 2018. Measuring Unpaid Care Work in Household Surveys. Research Report, Oxfam. www.oxfam.org.uk/policyandpractice.
Rubery, J. 2015. Regulating for Gender Equality: A Policy Framework to Support the Universal Caregiver Vision. *Social Politics* 22 (4): 513–538.
Rummery, K., and M. Fine. 2012. Care: A Critical Review of Theory, Policy and Practice. *Social Policy & Administration* 46 (3): 321–343. Published Online June 2012. https://doi.org/10.1111/j.1467-9515.2012.00845.x.
Rushton, S. 2010. AIDS and International Security in the United Nations System. *Health Policy and Planning* 25 (6): 495–504.
Ryan, C., and H. Basini. 2017. UNSC Resolution 1325 National Action Plans in Liberia and Sierra Leone: An Analysis of Gendered Power Relations in Hybrid Peacebuilding. *Journal of Intervention and Statebuilding* 11 (2): 189–217.
Sebhatu, R.W. 2017. (En)gendering Youth for Gender-Just Peace with UN Security Council Resolution 2250. Gender-Just Peace and Transitional Justice, No. 3, Lund University.
Shulika, L.S., and L. Shulika. 2016. Women and Peace Building: From Historical to Contemporary African Perspectives. *Ubuntu: Journal of Conflict Transformation* 5 (1): 7–31.
Sikod, Fo. 2007. Gender Division of Labour and Women's Decision-Making Power in Rural Households in Cameroon. *Africa Development* XXXII (3): 58–71. Council for the Development of Social Science Research in Africa (CODESRIA), Dakar.
Siem, F.F. 2017. Leaving Them Behind Healthcare Services in Situations of Armed Conflict. *Tidsskrift for Den Norske Legeforening* 137 (17): 1341–1343.
Stuart, S. 2014. Situation of Unpaid Work and Gender in the Caribbean: The Measurement of Unpaid Work Through Time—Use Studies. United Nations (ECLAC). Studies and Perspectives Series No. 34, The Caribbean.
Tavero, I.L., E.G. García, J.M. Seda, R.R. Serrano, I.M.C. Cabrera, and A.A. Rodríguez. 2018. The Gender Perspective in the Opinions and Discourse of Women About Caregiving. *Rev Esc Enferm USP* 52. Published Online 22 October 2018. https://doi.org/10.1590/s1980-220x2017009403370.

Thompson, M. 2006. Women, Gender, and Conflict: Making the Connections. *Development in Practice* 16 (3/4): 342–353.

Tønnessen, L., and S. Al-Nagar. 2013. The Women's Quota in Conflict Ridden Sudan: Ideological Battles for and Against Gender Equality. *Women's Studies International Forum* 41 (2): 122–131. Published Online November 2013. https://doi.org/10.1016/j.wsif.2013.03.006.

UNDP. 2015. Imbalances in Paid and Unpaid Work. Chapter 4 in UNDP Human Development Report 2015, Work for Human Development, New York.

UNSCR. 2000. United Nations Security Council Resolution 1325 on Women, Peace and Security (S/Res/1325). New York: United Nations. http://www.un.org/events/res_1325e.pdf.

UNSCR. 2008. United Nations Security Council Resolution 1820 on Women, Peace and Security (2008). https://undocs.org/en/S/RES/1820(2008).

UN—United Nations. 2009. Security Council Urges Renewed Measures to Improve Women's Participation in Peace Processes, Reaffirming Key Role Women Can Play in Rebuilding War-Torn Societies. Security Council Meeting SC/9759, 5 October 2009.

UN—United Nations. 2010. The World's Women 2010: Trends and Statistics. United Nations, Department of Economic and Social Affairs, Statistics Division, New York, Sales No. E.10.XVII.11. https://unstats.un.org/unsd/demographic/products/Worldswomen/WW_full%20report_color.pdf.

WHO. 2011. World Report on Disability 2011, World Health Organization, Malta. https://www.who.int/disabilities/world_report/2011/report.pdf.

Woodroffe, J., and K. Donald. 2014. Unpaid Care: A Priority for the Post-2015 Development Goals and Beyond. Gender and Development Network, Briefings 6.

Yavorsky, J.E., C.M. Kamp-Dush, and S.J. Schoppe-Sullivan. 2015. The Production of Inequality: The Gender Division of Labor Across the Transition to Parenthood. *Journal of Marriage & Family* 77 (3): 662–679.

Zembylas, M., V. Bozalek, and T. Shefer. 2014. Tronto's Notion of Privileged Irresponsibility and the Re-conceptualization of Care: Implications for Critical Pedagogies of Emotion in Higher Education Gender and Education. http://dx.doi.org/10.1080/09540253.2014.901718.

CHAPTER 4

The Ethics of Care and the Conceptualization of Unpaid Care Work

4.1 The Definition of Care Work and Its Related Concepts

"Care" in everyday language is an activity essential for the sustenance of life. It has given rise to an extensive body of literature, and has diverse meanings according to the field of study: sociology, social policy, feminist scholarship, morality, and in healthcare studies (especially with disability and ageing).

The use of the term "care" is extremely broad, applied at the interpersonal and global levels (Lloyd 2006). Caring is physically and mentally demanding but if this work is performed without any reference to an emotional bond and a normative context, it cannot be called care (Kröger 2009: 401). Care is the provision (in the household and the community) of time, attention, and support to meet the physical, mental, and social needs of the growing child and other household members (Engle et al. 1999). "Care" serves people's well-being, and includes both personal care and care-related activities (Fälth and Blackden 2009). Reddy et al. (2014: 4) put forward three general characteristics of care: it is an action, a mental state, and a moral value. Care is better understood as relationships that are constructed in culture and society, and shaped by political and structural environments (Green 2012). Held (2005) defines care as a practice and a value that is extended by caring persons who are not only motivated to care and participate in effective practices of care

F. O. Ibnouf, *War-Time Care Work and Peacebuilding in Africa*, Gender, Development and Social Change,
https://doi.org/10.1007/978-3-030-26195-5_4

but are compelled by moral salience of attending to and meeting the needs of the particular others for whom they take responsibility (cited in Chisale 2018). According to Peterson, care work refers to all the necessary activities performed to reproduce human life at personal and community levels where human life is generated and daily maintained (2002). It is a group of activities that serves people's well-being, the market and/or governments through a combination of paid and unpaid activities (Maestre and Thorpe 2016). Tronto (1993) sees it as a general activity, which includes collective care, rather than a dyadic one existing between two people—a caregiver and a dependent receiver—which Carol Gilligan (1982) and Noddings (2002) envisaged as being emblematic of the caring relationship. Tronto (2013) observes that caring very rarely happens only between a single caregiver and a receiver, but is more complex, even in the family milieu, where multiple people are caring for each other. Thus, there are various schools of thought with different points of views, analyses, and policies regarding care work.

Rummery and Fine (2012) reveals that there are three clearly distinguishable facets: first, care is understood as a feeling or emotion involving a disposition towards others, this appears as a personal concern for the well-being of one or more others. A second and distinct facet of care is the work and physical activity involved, this perspective sees care as a form of labour, tending to the needs of another. In the third facet, care is understood as a social relationship, also serves to distinguish care from other forms of work (ibid.). Sevenhuijsen puts relation in the centre of her definition of care when she argues that care is a concrete political activity that sees responsibilities as the very basis for our existence (Sevenhuijsen 2000 cited in Stensöta 2011). Tronto expands these types of relationships to the environment when she argues that care is "a species activity that includes everything that we do to maintain, continue and repair our world so that we can live in it as well as possible" (Tronto 1995). The notion of care is a valuable political concept and that how we think about care is deeply implicated in existing structures of power and inequality (Tronto 1993: 21).

Some scholars emphasize the moral dimension of caregiving (care work). Caregiving is a practice of empathic imagination, responsibility, witnessing, and solidarity with those in great need. For Kleinman, it is a moral practice that makes caregivers, and at times even the care receivers, more present and thereby fully human (2009). It connects people and imbues these connections with a wide range of emotions (Lawson

2007). Noddings believe emotion has a positive role to play in morality, but both are careful to qualify their claims. Noddings claims that caring receptivity for the other requires "feeling and sensitivity" but that emotion alone cannot ensure caring (cited in Hamington 2010). Gasper and Truong (2008) define care structures and human relationships. They make it possible to define care to the extent that we can see how it shapes our society. Power (2013) refers to Marion Barnes' argument that recognizes that care can help as a moral compass for the messy moral dilemmas that often arise when support is needed. The essential element, however, is to be able to recognize the need of the other and to act accordingly. For that reason, practical action represents an important dimension in care approach, together with a relational and a moral dimension (Martinsen 2011). Care is thus a trinity: "relational, practical and moral simultaneously" (ibid.). The practice of care is central to developing an ethic of care. Care refers both to certain practices and to certain values by which to evaluate those practices (Held 2006). Thus, care as ethics is developed through care as practice; the two can therefore never be wholly held apart (Sander-Staudt 2006).

In the caring concept, society values both caretakers and caregivers and recognizes their rights as human beings (Kingston 2007). The caregiver has been defined by Floriano et al. (2012) as a relative or a close relation, with no training in health, who is taking care of his or her family member.

The fact that there is no general consensus over the definition of caregiving makes attempts to measure the concept difficult. Even though a number of instruments related to the concept are available, they do not measure caregiving itself. Rather, they attempt to measure the effects of caregiving, that is, the burden, demands, impact, and distress, etc. (Hermanns and Mastel-Smith 2012). The burden of care is an emerging concept in the literature that describes the physical, emotional, social, and financial problems that can be experienced by family caregivers (O'Neill and Ross 1991). The burden of caregivers oftentimes refers to the informal caregivers' burden (Diameta et al. 2018). The term care work itself has several definitions and is used in many different ways. This work is time-consuming and, in many cases, physically demanding. Care work is often differentiated from other types of work because it is intrinsically linked to labour undertaken out of a sense of duty, responsibility, and love/affection, that is, it is often viewed as an emotionally driven occupation (Stuart 2014).

Unpaid care work is separated into three types of work. Most United Nations publications use the term "unpaid care work" quite broadly, synonymously with terms such as "nonmarket work" or the work of "social reproduction" (Folbre 2006). Budlender (2010: 4) states that the International Classification of Activities for Time Use Survey's (ICATUS) distinguishes three sub-categories, namely (unpaid) household maintenance, (unpaid) care for persons in one's own household, and (unpaid) community services to help other households. Providing and receiving care are central components of social life, as they accompany us over our entire life courses (Barnes 2012).

There is debate on care work and the public and private divide, although "private" and "public" are difficult to disentangle in connection to the ethics of care at the institutional levels of public and private domain of society. To state it differently, gender roles relate women to private and men to public domains, thus separating "private" from "public" domains. It means roles are gendered even if both domains and the interdependence with each other. Razavi and Silke (2012) argue that feminist scholarship on the gendered construction of welfare provisioning and welfare regimes has produced a conceptually strong and empirically grounded analysis of care, reinforcing the necessity of rethinking the distinctions between "the public" and "the private" as well as the links between them. Stensöta (2011) insists that women's emotions and care have been bounded to the private sphere, leaving the public and the decisions affecting both spheres to men, rationality and "non-care". The public and private spheres may be seen as different sides of the same coin, since care is provided within the household as well; it is a public policy concern to the society—care produces life and well-being to satisfy the human needs.

The care can be intimate, familial, and enduring, but may also be occupational or professional, limited in time and focused primarily or exclusively on mental and physical well-being (Rummery and Fine 2012). The term "caregiving" is widely used and has been studied from a variety of scientific perspectives, including nursing, sociology, and psychology (Hermanns and Mastel-Smith 2012). However, Hermanns and Mastel-Smith (2012) developed the following working definition, caregiving is made up of actions one does on behalf of another individual who is unable to do those actions for himself or herself. Schofield et al. (1998) define caregivers as "people who are under obligation to care because of their close kinship or emotional bond with the care recipients".

How has feminism contributed to the concept of care? Feminists are often concerned with the ways in which care is often a feminized work. The feminization of care is thus connected to the traditional principal that women are responsible as family caregiver/provider. Most feminists focus substantially on carers, particularly family carers, and on caregiving (Rummery and Fine 2012). Seeing women so often when looking through the lens of care, because women shoulder the majority of the world's care work burden and their moral agency tends to be characterized by practices of care towards particular others (Robinson 2011: 9). Worldwide women typically spend disproportionately more time on unpaid care work than men (Ferrant et al. 2014). The feminization of care responsibilities and the time women devote to these responsibilities result in subordinate position women occupy in economic and political life, thus perpetuating asymmetric gender relations (Eyben 2012). Caregivers are overwhelming feminine in the noble aspiration to care for and to reduce economic, physical, and emotional burdens for their families and community. Female caregivers bear more burdened than male caregivers (Marks et al. 2002). Tradition and culture influences men and women interests, relations, and needs. It determines how people associate within their family and in their society. In some cultures, women (mother, sister, wife, daughter, and females in-laws) are responsible for more care work and domestic activities than men. Thus, care work is a mechanism that shapes the division of labour at home by gender. It is no surprise then that the analysis of care has been most developed by feminists (Razavi and Silke 2012).

Is caregiving a natural instinct and the root cause of inequality? Care responsibilities have been "feminized" and degraded by gender norms in a variety of contexts (Robinson 2011: 9). Gender roles are essential for understanding care work. Women are required to meet their respective societal expectations unlike men. Most African cultures function along patriarchal lines which undermine the intelligence, dignity, and value of women—women being half of their population. Most norms and assumptions have long taken for granted. Where cultural and traditional values are still strongly respected, gender roles are extremely visible. Gender roles are not innate or static but a consequence of social and cultural factors. These roles are widely understood as referring to social roles and responsibilities that are assigned by society to a male or a female within their society. Gendered values, norms, and practices are much deeply ingrained in women and in society as a whole that it takes active awareness to recognize them on a daily basis. Women are blindly loyal to their deep-seated beliefs. For instance, traditional practices that violate the rights of women persist because they are not questioned or challenged and therefore take on an aura of morality in the eyes of those practising them (Maluleke 2012). Tradition is often misinterpreted or skewed towards patriarchal satisfaction which leads to gender inequality. Gender equality is a non-issue to those who are not directly conscious of its significance. Unpaid care work lies at the heart of persistent gender inequality and acts as a barrier to women's economic empowerment.[1]

The different understandings of care have concrete effects in shaping different policy agendas (Eyben 2012). Depending on the way care is framed, policies and practices can be designed and implemented in transformative ways to supporting carers—predominantly women—and lightening their care burdens, while challenging the notion that this work is intrinsically "female" and of lesser importance than work seen to be more "productive" (Esquivel 2014). Where policies have been implemented, translating these policies into practical projects remains a major challenge.

4.2 The Conceptualization of Wartime Care Work

The concept of care is gaining grounds in academic research and policy making. Conceptually and theoretically, care work has been subject to different interpretations and has several different definitions. However, these definitions have not been taken into account the complexity and difficulty of everyday practices of care work in armed conflict and post conflict contexts, since wartime care is of particular importance to the survival of war-affected populations, as it can be seen in Darfur. While unpaid care work is not conceived as a man's responsibility, women are considered to be caregivers. Women by "nature" are caregivers and moral keepers—such patriarchal beliefs continue to shape wartime care work practices. Thus, caregiving is gendered, with women as most of the caregivers. This stereotype is amplified during conflict.

As far as care ethics from a feminist perspective is concerned, it is difficult to identify care needs for different contexts and social situations. Also, the lived realities and experiences of those affected by conflict needs are to be considered. The everyday care practices are subjected to the needs and contexts of individuals. During war, people have different needs, which require different types of care in order to survive everyday dangers. Care as compassion and responsiveness to need, care is vital for people living during and after armed conflict. Thus, care contributes to elevate people's well-being, physically, emotionally, and psychologically. Even though some feminists' postulate that women are expected to bear the brunt of caregiving responsibilities during wartime, carers/caregivers are more likely to face more challenges in arranging care due to the war context. Wartime care work involves drudgery and overwork and unpaid care becomes even more arduous and an extremely heavy burden in armed conflict context. As indicated by Orozco and Dominguez (2014), care is comprised of all those activities necessary to recreate the physical and emotional well-being of people. Care arrangements must be rendered active during and in the aftermath war to maximize the chances of survival in harsh and horrific situations. In these situations, demand for care increases in terms of quality and quantity as a result of higher prevalence of disability, wounded people and of HIV/AIDS demanding care daily.

In this book, care work refers to care work in wartime and post-war periods. This book adopts the concept of "care" put forward by Orozco and Leiras (2017), namely "activities that serve, on a daily basis, to enhance or sustain life; the life of all people as interdependent subjects and in any social context". The book re-conceptualizes care work as a specialized activity in wartime that is difficult to research, but one that makes women a specific kind of protagonists whose knowledge and perspective are necessary to better understand the nature of armed conflicts and the structures that contribute to survival and well-being of the communities during war and in post-armed conflict conditions. Care work includes all of the functions performed by women as caregivers/providers in armed conflict and post-armed conflict situations. But, what does wartime care work involve? It encompasses women's daily arrangements for the provision of basic necessities to ensure the survival; emotional and psychological support; care for children/adolescents, elderly, disabled/sick; heal the wounded, care for the dying, and protect family members and maintaining their health. As Bakker (2007) contends, care work includes all the essential tasks, for example, childcare, cooking, and cleaning required to supporting the development of cognitive, emotional, and physical capabilities of people. In short, wartime care work is embedded in everything and everything worth something takes preparation. Almost all care activities during and after war are essential for the child growth, family survival and well-being, and community solidarity and resilience.

In the book *The Heart of Justice: Care Ethics and Political Theory*, Daniel Engster (2007) defines caring as "… everything we do directly to help individuals to meet their vital biological needs, develop or maintain their basic capabilities, and avoid or alleviate unnecessary or unwanted pain and suffering, so that they can survive, develop, and function in society" (cited in Friedman 2009). Care work involves offering physical, psychological, and emotional support, in addition to the protection and maintenance of family relations. It has an associated emotional response and it influences how people act towards others around them in such difficult circumstances. In all its forms, care work benefits the society on the whole (ILO 2007) by providing the daily material, emotional, and social support upon which survival, work, and social life depend.

4.3 Ethics of Wartime Care Work

The theoretical approach for this book borrows from various theories developed within the ethics of care approach, with particular attention to Fiona Robinson (2011). Since the early 1980s, the ethics of care began to emerge and has become a theoretical tool of great importance within care research. "An ethics of care" is the most common theoretical perspective used within the research on care. Although ethical care is not originally a feminist concept, feminists have enhanced its usefulness by highlighting the value of fundamental moral obligations to self and others. Fiona Robinson (2011: 17) credits Hekman (1997: 361) to summarize that the aim of ethics of care "[is] not to uncover a new or more complete or better truth" but to "create a set of ideal types that allow us to 'see' a different world". Overtime, the development of feminist ethics of care thinking has generated different perspectives. Many feminists and theorists of ethics of care thinking have raised concerns for women's conditions in diverse areas of society; aided in developing a "women-centred practice"; highlighted "women's distinct voice and identity"; brought to light "feminization of care", shaded light on the issues of power "domination and subordination"; and celebrated "women's diversity" and focused more on "questions of morality and rationality". More recently, there have been moves towards what is known as ethics of care and social (and also human) security, that is, the ethics of care to achieve justice and well-being within policy and practice. Fiona Robinson's ethic of care (2011) is an example of how to understand the responsibilities of sustaining life that is central to the struggle for basic human security using a feminist ethic of care lens. Moreover, the research on political philosophy of the ethics of care continues to develop.

The key aspects of the feminist care theory are used as the cornerstone in the case study carried out in Darfur. A feminist ethics of care allows for a consideration of the lived experiences of those affected by war in a meaningful way. This is a matter of concern for women as caregivers in armed conflict. During wartime and in the aftermath of war, women expand their role to arrange for all types of life-saving care work. Thus, the care burden is multiplied exponentially under such specific situations. Conceptually, to study unpaid care work from a feminist perspective enables a specific account of women's subjectivities both in war and peace times. The feminist perspective has the added benefit of challenging misunderstandings on the various roles performed by women as caregivers in building and sustaining peace. This concretely analyse the theoretical frameworks and makes the knowledge and experiences of marginalized women in conflict situations a focal point. There is no specific formula and no one method of achieving sustainable peace. But more importantly, there is a need to infuse the practical experiences of affected populations in a way that often mirrors real life to bring about more reflective, effective, and innovative peacebuilding processes. Some scholars view ethics of care as either a practice, moral virtue, methodology, or a combination of these. Theorists with an emphasis on the centrality of responsibility are very different from theorists with justice-oriented ethics. The contemporary growing body of research on ethics of care has evolved from the work of psychologist Carol Gilligan (Stensöta 2011).

The deeply embedded cultural beliefs and ethical values contribute to gender bias in the burden of caregiving. However, during and in the aftermath of war, women are more affected than men as they tend to offer more hours of unpaid caregiving for the survival of their family members. Thus, caregiving arrangements have fallen disproportionately on women with limited resources and absence of basic care services. Their commitment as caregivers is embedded in the ethical standards within their traditional societies. Women take on most of the everyday caregiving responsibilities however, women feel more responsible and obliged to fulfil their duty as caregivers/providers. Women and men internalize gender norms and come to view caring as women's work (Swinkels et al. 2017). Engster points out that "there is a moral obligation to care when others cannot reasonably meet their needs on their own" (cited in Friedman 2009).

Women have been socialized to take over the care responsibilities. Feminist scholars have drawn attention to gendered aspect of care provision. Such as Bondi (2008) who describes how caring work is "given" to women and that this often becomes a defining characteristic of their self-identity and lifework. Men are discouraged from doing "women's work", as if it is inherently of less value (Wong et al. 2012). However, as Liera and Saraceno (2002) argue, care work was invisible when it was interpreted as something intrinsically female. The issues of care, culture, well-being, and practices of responsibilities are inextricably linked. The amount of unpaid care work carried out has important implications for the well-being of individuals and households (Budlender 2010). During and in the aftermath of war, women shoulder most of the burden of unpaid care work without adequate support services, when most of these women and girls are in need of help themselves.

At the centre of the ethics of care theory is a network of human interdependence, challenging the public/private divide, and a focus on the values arising from refocusing on interdependence (Hankivsky 2004 cited in Clough 2015). Care ethics emphasizes on empathy, relations, and responsibility, in addition to the moral value of care practice. Care has also been argued to constitute an ethical foundation for social theory and research which points directly to the importance of connectivity and active collaboration (Held 2007 cited in Blazek et al. 2015: 46). Held asserts that "morality should address issues of caring and empathy and relationships between people rather than only or primarily the rational decisions of solitary moral agents" (1995 cited in Whyte and Cuomo 2016). The work of educational psychologist Carol Gilligan's (1982) in her famous book *In a Different Voice* provided the impetus for the development of ethics of care theory. Gilligan (1982) suggests that the ethics of care is rooted in the moral frameworks of responsibility and relationships rather than rights and rules and that any care orientation is inseparable from contextual circumstances rather than being a formal and abstract system of thought. Additionally, care is grounded in the daily activity of life rather that a set of universal principles (cited in Green 2012).

4.4 A Feminist Ethics of Care in African Context

Another theme explained in this part of the chapter is the ethics of care work in African culture and its connection with ethics of care. Some academics argue that ethics of care theories originating from the West are not suitable to meet the needs of either indigenous or working-class people, thus they have expressed a need for contextually relevant theories that are derived from the experiences of those who are marginalized in their specific environment. Care itself may be considered universally but the specificity of local context/cultures and social relations that frame ethical choices. At this point, this book has yet to come across a feminist ethics of care theory that was developed in Africa. While women in the West have fought for their place in society resulting in developing "the ethics of care", women from Africa are still struggling to find their feet (Mangena 2009).

Although African cultures display awesome diversity, they also show remarkable similarities (Lutz 2009). This is also affirmed by Metz and Gaie (2010) that "in Africa while there is substantial diversity among its traditional cultures, there are also threads that many share". The ethic of Ubuntu is unique to Africa and is observed in most countries in Africa. According to Van Binsbergen (2001), Ubuntu is a revived African concept that does not only focus on a particular locality or region, but rather on the entire continent. Literature indicates that Ubuntu is not necessarily under the same name in the whole of Africa, but is similar in different countries of the continent, for example, "Ubuntu" in Uganda and Tanzania, and "Unhu" in Zimbabwe, "Botho" in Botswana, but the meaning remains the same. "Ubuntu" is broadly defined as an "African worldview" that places communal interests above those of the individual, and where human existence is dependent upon interaction with others, Ubuntu is a long-standing tradition on the continent (McDonald 2010). The ethical tradition of African life is "Ubuntu" and the spirit of Ubuntu is prevalent in most African cultures; this is a common trait in traditional African society, where people from the same community support each other (Metz and Gaie 2010). Ubuntu has become synonymous with care ethics (Chisale 2018). Similarly, Waghid and Smeyers (2012) defined Ubuntu as the principle of care. The social character of African ethics is affiliated to notions of the ethics of duty (not of rights) (Gyekye 2010). Central to the ethics of care is the belief that relations and practices of care and responsibility are the basic substance of morality and that these relations and practices are a central feature of all human social life (Robinson 2011). Ubuntu "an African philosophical way of life" is a revitalization of African values and moral principles (Mapaure 2011). The dominant theme of African cultures is that the life of another person is at least as valuable as one's own (Mapaure 2011). In contrast, the tenets of feminist care theory stress that all human beings exist in relation to others and that different types and levels of power frame their experiences of [in]security (Robinson 2011). For this reason, a care ethic will pay attention to how global (e.g. globalization) as well as national (e.g. armed conflicts) events impact the lives of people.

Caregiving functions are presumed to be feminine by culture and they summarize the philosophy of Ubuntu (Chisale 2018). Ubuntu is an act of caring in the society. Eltigani (1995) noted that traditional societies in Western Sudan have a system of generalized reciprocity to deal with crisis and to support group welfare. In its original conception, the ethics of care emphasized the moral duty that is attached to caring for someone. The ethics of care emphasizes the moral importance of our ties to our family and other groups (Held 2006). Thus, the ethics of care focuses on the cluster of values involved in fostering and maintaining caring relations—values such as trust, empathy, sensitivity, mutual considerations, solidarity, and responsiveness to need (Held 2006). Care ethics involves valuing empathy and emotion over rules and rights (Hamington 2010).

African cultures are embedded in strong moral considerations. It is true that Africa is inhabited by various ethnic nationalities, but in spite of their various cultures, Africans do share some dominant traits in their belief systems and have similar values that mark them out from other peoples of the world (Idang 2015). Both traditions and religious beliefs are shaping values and cultural attitudes towards caregiving in Muslim and Christian communities in Africa. Values are an integral part of culture and culture is what defines a people's identity, it does appear that cultures always try to maintain those values that are necessary for the survival of their people (Idang 2015). In African cultures, humanity is viewed as collective rather than as individuals and that this collective view is expressed as a shared concern and responsibility for the well-being of others (Lutz 2009). Caregiving is often shaped by cultural norms and expectation. Values, beliefs, and behaviours can and should be described with reference to caregiving. The social and cultural construction of masculinity and femininity that assigns caring responsibility to women is deeply embedded in the socio-cultural, moral, and affective values, learned in early childhood. Caregiving is culturally embedded, that is, accepted by women unquestioned. Even women themselves are socialized to internalize these practices and participate in their provision. In Africa, caregiving responsibilities extend beyond the nuclear family and encompass extended family members, infirm elderly relatives and non-relatives.

Ubuntu protects human relationships. The Ubuntu philosophy is "a person becoming a person in relation with other persons" (Waghid and Smeyers 2012). Care is an attitude towards others, be the nuclear or extended family, or community at large. Metz and Gaie (2010) assert that the African concept of justice which is represented in Ubuntu can be reduced to transcend the ethic of care's perspectives, relationality and reciprocity of care model. Thus both "care" and "Ubuntu" demand that a person transcends from individualism into collective engagement in care during and after armed conflict. In Africa, community caregiving is one of the traditional aspects of cooperation in rural communities and it is considered an effective social solidarity mechanism. African customs and traditions are intrinsically linked to the extended family. Predominantly in rural areas the household consists of the extended family, and family relations in traditional societies is based on ties of kinship and affinity. There is a type of community and kinship solidarity, which is a reciprocal arrangement between people locally. This form of solidarity is based on traditional values and is important in binding and strengthening ties within the community.

4.5 The Research Methodology

The field survey sheds light on the true "lived experiences" of "caregivers" within the context of conflict and post-conflict settings. The care ethic approach demands an accurate understanding of the situation on the ground. Many difficulties and challenges are involved in conducting research in conflict area, such as, insecurity, ethical and methodological complexities and restrictions associated with conducting fieldwork on people affected by war and forced displacement. To capture the complexity, diversity, and plurality of the women's experiences, and to minimize problems associated with one method, this study utilized a judicious mixed of qualitative and quantitative data collection methods in the field. Mixed methods are able to grasp wartime care work arrangements in all their variety as moral and human relations. This research study makes use of quantitative and qualitative methods and procedures to provide a complete picture of women as caregivers/providers during and after the war in Darfur. As Abowitz and Toole (2010) highlight, the utility of applying a mixed-methods research approach enhances the reliability and validity of the results as it allows the researcher to balance the strengths and weaknesses of each approach. In development studies, a judicious combination of qualitative and quantitative methods can help solve problems that are associated with each method employed separately (Kanbur 2001; White 2002). Moreover, Gorard and Taylor (2004) contend that the research claims become stronger if the data come from a variety of methods and the results may be more persuasive and convincing to policy-makers. The structured and un-structured interviews together with focus group discussions and storytelling serve as a rich primary source of data. The research also uses secondary data that is already publicly available such as Government and national and international non-governmental organizations' reports, records, statistics, and working papers and field surveys. Finally, two academic workshops were held with experts in the field to discuss the preliminary findings and to get feedback on the project. The participants were drawn from academia, research centres, civil society organizations, women association, NGOs and UN agencies, among others. Relevant points raised during the workshop were integrated into this work.

This study raises questions concerning the extent to which peace actors are aware of the realities of unpaid care work arrangements in armed conflict and post-armed conflict situations. The empirical study analyses the following questions: what role do women as care providers play in the complex dynamics of wartime and in the aftermath of war? Do women as caregivers bear most of the burden? What is a caregiver life experience during "wartime" and in the absence of war? What challenges do they face in the upkeep of IDPs? What links exist between caregiving arrangement and peacebuilding? This study takes a look at the mechanism of wartime caregiving: Who is responsible for giving/providing care during and in the aftermath of war? How does care work during armed conflict and post-armed conflict settings impact the role of women as caregivers? And most importantly, how do the silenced voices of women as care providers situate them in the peacebuilding processes? What would be the proposal by women as caregivers, should they be granted audience? What measures can be taken to ensure the meaningful inclusion of caregivers' needs and priorities in peacebuilding processes? It does not matter whoever is leading the change if there is no clear vision about how to bring the valuable experiences of wartime caregiving into the peacebuilding process. Why are the different experiences, priorities, and perspective of caregivers in wartime and after war needed in armed conflict transformation and post-armed conflict reconstruction? These questions, which support the research, effectively raise the essential concerns about how care arrangements by women during and after war might offer the enabling environment for building peace in Sudan, as well as in Africa. Thus, the research contributes to an in-depth understanding of the women's diverse experiences of care work arrangement and the challenges they deal with daily during wartime and in post-armed conflict situation. Women, as caregivers, are powerful agents of peace and their efforts need recognition, valuation, visibility, and support.

The case study research method was used in conducting the research in Darfur. Case study application to a specific piece of research has given the appropriate subject matter, context, and research aims, shown it to be a method as credible and robust as other approaches (Yin 2003). Moreover, case study research allows the researcher to secure insights through a variety of perspectives (Van der Velde et al. 2004). Within the case, multiple research methods were employed in anticipation of providing a more complete picture on women as care providers during and after war in Darfur. The following data collection methods were employed: structured questionnaire, open-ended interviews, focus group discussions, interviews with key informants, and storytelling. Structured and unstructured interviews and the focus group-guided questions were designed after a review of the relevant literature (for example, Bryman 2001; Rabiee 2004; Liamputtong 2011). These methods were corroborated with direct observation, where possible, women (in the sample) were observed during their performing of multiple care work activities. The data collection methods were piloted first and revised in the field. Interviews and notes were carried out in Arabic and then translated as precisely as possible to English language for this book. All interviews with participants' consent were audio taped for further analysis. The interviews were also conducted face-to-face because of the high level of illiteracy, and poverty particularly among displaced women which renders them incapable owning and using communication devices.

Darfur state government in collaboration with UN agencies have established a number of camps located in the areas with relatively stable security conditions. The internally displaced people (IDP) camps are in need of water and sanitation facilities, among others, and operate with limited supplies to prevent illnesses and epidemics. Elsewhere in Africa, it has been reported that IDPs do not usually have access to basic services such as food, potable water, decent housing, and schools (Oginni et al. 2018). In order to capture a variety of caregivers lived experiences during wartime, respondents were selected from five different IDP camps. The study was conducted in Zamzam and Abu-Shook in Northern Darfur and Otash, Kalma, and El-Sereif in Southern Darfur which represent the five largest IDP camps in the Darfur region. Some of these IDP camps have slowly become permanent settlements (such as El-Sereif becoming "El-Sereif City"), while Kalma camp (the largest camp in South Darfur State) probably will become a town on its own. Many IDP camps initially are expected to be temporary, but it is clear some will become permanent settlement. The surveyed sample of this study included displaced women in IDPs camps, traditional leaders in charge of IDPs camps, and humanitarian agencies and local women's groups, CSOs' and NGOs' personnel and government officials involved in supporting and serving IDPs. The participants signed or finger-printed on the information consent forms. Photographs were taken and videos were recorded with participants' consent. The participants were informed of the purposes for the study and on how much of their limited time is needed.

War causes a lot of damages but also makes strong people. Storytelling offered women the opportunity to communicate their care work experiences, thoughts, and their painful feelings verbally. Most described their painful displacement journeys, the murder of their beloved one(s), the destruction of their property, injuries sustained by close relatives, etc. They are in a constant state of insecurity themselves and their family members too. They all told different stories of their experiences and challenges as caregivers. Bell (2009: 109) asserts that stories have individual and collective purposes, giving us the chance to talk about issues perceived not to be our reality, or that we are afraid to admit as being part of our lives, such as racism.

A four-step process of the thematic analysis of qualitative data (Braun and Clarke 2006) was used. These stages were: coding, theme identification, theme organization, and description. The transcriptions were coded in relation to the guided questions, and then analysed through the data compilation of participant responses. The main ideas and most important points that were expressed for each category/theme that was identified and classified. Then the key findings under each main theme or category presented using appropriate precise quotes to illustrate the findings. The quotations used in this study are verbatim and are presented in italics. The findings are then critically discussed alongside their practical implications. This is followed by realistic conclusions and recommendations for a variety of peace practitioners and a framework for policymaking.

The link between wartime care work arrangements and peacebuilding processes will be explored further through the making of a short documentary film. The title of documentary is **"Count me in!"** This short documentary would bring into focus the issues of women and care work arrangement during wartime and in post-conflict. It presents the opportunity to share ground-breaking stories that makes the voices of the silenced heard, which can be used to better inform policy and post-conflict reconstruction efforts. The film goes from the normal scope of interviewing and research to produce an incredibly moving story on wartime care work. There is a need to listen to the voices of caregivers who are at work on the frontlines of communities at wartime and in post-conflict to ensure the survival of millions. Building peace implies placing the processes of sustaining daily life in the centre of the peacebuilding process. The documentary film will be useful for all peacebuilders because it is based on actual parameters.

Note

1. Briefings 2017—Sharing the load Unpaid care work and women's economic empowerment. https://static1.squarespace.com/static/536c4ee8e4b0b60bc6ca7c74/t/5899e0316b8f5bbffd74b7d4/1486479412285/GADN+Sharing+the+load+briefing+2017+final.pdf.

Bibliography

Abowitz, D.A., and T.M. Toole. 2010. Mixed-Method Research: Fundamental Issues of Design, Validity, and Reliability in Construction Research. *Journal of Construction Engineering and Management* 136 (1): 108–116.

Bakker, I. 2007. Social Reproduction and the Constitution of a Gendered Political Economy. *New Political Economy* 12 (4): 541–556.

Barnes, M. 2012. *Care in Everyday Life: An Ethic of Care in Practice*. Bristol: Policy Press.

Bell, L.A. 2009. The Story of the Storytelling Project: An Arts-Based Race and Social Justice Curriculum. *Storytelling, Self, Society* 5 (2): 107–118.

Blazek, M., F.M. Smith, M. Lemešová, and P. Hricová. 2015. Ethics of Care Across Professional and Everyday Positionalities: The (Un)expected Impacts of Participatory Video with Young Female Carers in Slovakia. *Geoforum* 61: 45–55.

Bondi, L. 2008. On the Relational Dynamics of Caring: A Psychotherapeutic Approach to Emotional and Power Dimensions of Women's Care Work. *Gender, Place & Culture* 15 (3): 249–265.

Braun, V., and V. Clarke. 2006. Using Thematic Analysis in Psychology. *Qualitative Research in Psychology* 3 (2): 77–101. ISSN 1478-0887. http://dx.doi.org/10.1191/1478088706qp063oa.

Budlender, D. 2010. *Time Use Studies and Unpaid Care Work*, 1st ed. New York: Routledge.

Bryman, A. 2001. *Social Research Methods*. Oxford: Oxford University Press.

Chisale, S.S. 2018. *Ubuntu* as Care: Deconstructing the Gendered *Ubuntu*. *Verbum et Ecclesia* 39 (1): 1–8. Published Online 14 May 2018. https://doi.org/10.4102/ve.v39i1.1790.

Clough, B. 2015. Exploring the Potential of Relational Approaches to Mental Capacity Law. PhD Thesis, University of Manchester, Faculty of Humanities, Manchester.

Diameta, E., I. Adandom, S.U. Jumbo, H.C. Nwankwo, P.C. Obi, and M.E. Kalu. 2018. The Burden Experience of Formal and Informal Caregivers of Older Adults with Hip Fracture in Nigeria. *Sage Open Nursing* 4: 1–10.

Eltigani, T.E. 1995. *War and Drought in the Sudan: Essay on Population Displacement*. Gainesville: University Press Florida.

Engle, P.L., P. Menon, and L. Haddad. 1999. Care and Nutrition: Concepts and Measurement. *World Development* 27 (8): 1309–1337.

Esquivel, V. 2014. What Is a Transformative Approach to Care, and Why Do We Need It? *Gender & Development* 22 (3): 423–439.

Eyben, R. 2012. The Hegemony Cracked: The Power Guide to Getting Care onto the Development Agenda. Working Paper, 411, 1–29, Institute of Development Studies (IDS), Brighton.

Fälth, A., and M. Blackden. 2009. Unpaid Care Work, Gender Equality and Poverty Reduction Policy Brief. Issue 1, UNDP, New York.

Ferrant, G., L.M. Pesando, and K. Nowacka. 2014. Unpaid Care Work: The Missing Link in the Analysis of Gender Gaps in Labor Outcomes. Issue Paper, OECD Development Center.

Floriano, L.A., R.C. Azevedo, A.A. Reiners, and M.R. Sudré. 2012. Care Performed by Family Caregivers to Dependent Elderly, at Home, Within the Context of the Family Health Strategy. *Texto Contexto Enferm* 21 (3): 543–548.

Folbre, N. 2006. Measuring Care: Gender, Empowerment, and the Care Economy. *Journal of Human Development* 7 (2): 183–199. Published Online 22 January 2007. https://doi.org/10.1080/14649880600768512.

Friedman, M. 2009. Review of Daniel Engster, The Heart of Justice: Care Ethics and Political Theory. *The Philosophical Review* 118 (2): 256–258. https://doi.org/10.1215/00318108-2008-048.

Gasper, D., and T. Truong. 2008. Development Ethics Through the Lenses of Caring, Gender, and Human Security. Working Paper, No. 459, Institute of Social Studies, Netherlands.

Gilligan, C. 1982. *In a Different Voice: Psychological Theory and Women's Development*. Cambridge, MA and Boston: Harvard University Press.

Gorard, S., and C. Taylor. 2004. *Combining Methods in Educational Research*. Maidenhead: Open University Press.

Green, B. 2012. Applying Feminist Ethics of Care to Nursing Practice. *Journal of Nursing and Care* 1 (3): 1–4. Published Online January 2012. https://doi.org/10.4172/2167-1168.1000111.

Gyekye, K. 2010. African Ethics. In *Stanford Encyclopedia of Philosophy*, ed. E.N. Zalta. Stanford: The Metaphysics Research Lab.

Hamington, M. 2010. Care Ethics, John Dewey's "Dramatic Rehearsal," and Moral Education. In *Philosophy of Education Yearbook*, 121–128. https://www.academia.edu.

Held, V. 2006. *The Ethics of Care: Personal, Political, and Global*. Oxford: Oxford University Press.

Hermanns, M., and B. Mastel-Smith. 2012. Caregiving: A Qualitative Concept Analysis. *The Qualitative Report* 17 (38): 1–18.

Hobbs, M.H., and C. Rice. 2018. *Gender and Women's Studies: Critical Terrain*, 2nd ed. Canada: Women's Press.

Idang, G.E. 2015. African Culture and Values. *Phronimon* 16 (2): 97–111. Online Version ISSN 1561-4018.

Kanbur, R. 2001. Qualitative and Quantitative Poverty Appraisal: The State of Play and Some Questions. Paper Presented at Qualitative and Quantitative Poverty Appraisal: Complementaries, Tensions and the Way Forward Workshop Held at Qualitative and Quantitative Poverty Appraisal, Cornell University, 15–16 March 2001.

Kingston, A.K. 2007. *Mothering Special Needs: A Different Maternal Journey*, 1st ed. London and Philadelphia: Jessica Kingsley.

Kleinman, A. 2009. Caregiving: The Odyssey of Becoming More Human. *The Lancet* 373 (9660): 292–293. Published Online 24 January 2009. https://doi.org/10.1016/S0140-6736(09)60087-8.

Kröger, T. 2009. Care Research and Disability Studies: Nothing in Common? *Critical Social Policy* 29 (3): 398–420. Published Online July 2009. https://doi.org/10.1177/0261018309105177.

Lawson, V. 2007. Geographies of Care and Responsibility. *Annals of the Association of American Geographers* 97 (1): 1–11.

Liamputtong, P. 2011. *Focus Group Methodology Principle and Practice*, 1st ed. London: Sage.

Liera, A., and C. Saraceno. 2002. Care: Actors, Relationships and Context. In *Contested Concepts in Gender and Social Politics*, ed. B. Hobson, J. Lewis, and B. Siim. Cheltenham, UK: Edward Elgar.

Lloyd, L. 2006. A Caring Profession? The Ethics of Care and Social Work with Older People. *British Journal of Social Work* 36: 1171–1185. Published Online November 2005. https://doi.org/10.1093/bjsw/bch400.

Lutz, D.W. 2009. African Ubuntu Philosophy and Global Management. *Journal of Business Ethics* 84 (Supplement 3: Global and Contextual Values for Business in a Changing World): 313–328.

Maestre, M., and J. Thorpe. 2016. *Understanding Unpaid Care Work to Empower Women in Market Systems Approaches.* London: The BEAM Exchange.

Maluleke, M.J. 2012. Culture, Tradition, Custom, Law and Gender Equality. *Potchefstroom Electronic Law Journal* 15 (1): 1–22. Published Online December 2011. https://doi.org/10.4314/pelj.v15i1.1.

Mangena, F. 2009. The Search for an African Feminist Ethic: A Zimbabwean Perspective. *Journal of International Women's Studies* 11 (2): 18–30.

Mapaure, C. 2011. Reinvigorating African Values for SADC: The Relevance of Traditional African Philosophy of Law in a Globalizing World of Competing Perspectives. *SADC Law Journal* 7: 149–173. ISSN 2222-288X (Online).

Marks, N.F., J.D. Lambert, and H. Choi. 2002. Transitions to Caregiving, Gender, and Psychological Well-Being: A Prospective U.S. National Study. *Journal of Marriage and Family* 64 (3): 657–667.

Martinsen, E.H. 2011. Care for Nurses Only? Medicine and the Perceiving Eye. *Health Care Analysis* 19 (1): 15–27. Published Online 7 December 2010. https://doi.org/10.1007/s10728-010-0161-9.

McDonald, D.A. 2010. Ubuntu Bashing: The Marketisation of 'African Values' in South Africa. *Review of African Political Economy* 37 (124): 139–152.

Metz, T., and J.B.R. Gaie. 2010. The African Ethic of Ubuntu/Botho: Implications for Research on Morality. *Journal of Moral Education* 39 (3): 273–290.

Noddings, N. 2002. *Starting at Home: Caring and Social Policy*, 1st ed. Berkeley, CA: University of California Press.

Oginni, S.O., M.P. Opoku, and B.A. Alupo. 2018. Terrorism in the Lake Chad Region: Integration of Refugees and Internally Displaced Persons. *Journal of Borderlands Studies* 33 (1): 315–316.

O'Neill, G., and M.M. Ross. 1991. Burden of Care: An Important Concept for Nurses. *Health Care for Women International* 12 (1): 11–21.

Orozco, A.P., and A.A. Leiras. 2017. *Why We Care About Care, An Essay Collection on Care Economy.* Booklet, UN Women Training Centre.

Orozco, A.P., and M.G. Dominguez. 2014. *Reading Paper Series on Care Economy: Chapter 1: Care: The Basic Concepts.* UN-Women Training Centre.

Peterson, V.S. 2002. Rewriting (Global) Political Economy as Reproductive, Productive, and Virtual (Foucauldian) Economies. *International Feminist Journal of Politics* 4 (1): 1–30.

Power, A. 2013. Care in Everyday Life: An Ethic of Care in Practice. *Disability & Society* 28 (8): 1176–1178. Published Online December 2013. https://doi.org/10.1080/09687599.2013.841623.

Rabiee, F. 2004. Focus-Group Interview and Data Analysis. *Proceedings of the Nutrition Society* 63 (4): 655–660. Published Online December 2004. https://doi.org/10.1079/pns2004399.

Razavi, S., and S. Silke. 2012. Introduction: Care Workers in the Global Economy: Worlds Apart? In *Global Variations in the Political and Social Economy of Care*. New York: Routledge.

Reddy, V., S. Meyer, T. Shefer, and T. Meyiwa. 2014. Towards a Critical Theory of Care. In *Care in Context: Transnational Gender Perspectives*, ed. V. Reddy, S. Meyer, T. Shefer, and T. Meyiwa, 1–27. Cape Town: HSRC Press.

Robinson, F. 2011. *The Ethics of Care: A Feminist Approach to Human Security*. Philadelphia: Temple University Press.

Rummery, K., and M. Fine. 2012. Care: A Critical Review of Theory, Policy and Practice. Social Policy & Administration 46 (3): 321–343. Published Online June 2012. https://doi.org/10.1111/j.1467-9515.2012.00845.x.

Sander-Staudt, M. 2006. The Unhappy Marriage of Care Ethics and Virtue Ethics. *Hypatia* 21 (4): 21–40.

Schofield, H., S. Bloch, H. Herrman, B. Murphy, J. Nankervis, and B. Singh (eds.). 1998. *Family Caregivers: Disability, Illness and Ageing*. St Leonards, NSW: Allen and Unwin in Association with VicHealth, the Victorian Health Promotion Foundation.

Sevenhuijsen, S., V. Bozalek, A. Gouws, and M. Minnar-McDonald. 2003. South African Social Welfare Policy: An Analysis Using the Ethic of Care. *Critical Social Policy* 23 (3): 299–321.

Stensöta, H.O. 2011. A Public Ethics of Care for Public Administration and Implementation. A Paper Presented at the Northwestern Political Science Conference, in San Antonio, Texas, April 20–22.

Stuart, S. 2014. Situation of Unpaid Work and Gender in the Caribbean: The Measurement of Unpaid Work Through Time—Use Studies. United Nations (ECLAC). Studies and Perspectives Series No. 34, The Caribbean.

Swinkels, J., T. van Tilburg, E. Verbakel, and M.B. van Groenou. 2017. Explaining the Gender Gap in the Caregiving Burden of Partner Caregivers. *Journal of Gerontology: Social Sciences* 74 (2): 309–317.

Tronto, J.T. 1993. *Moral Boundaries: A Political Argument for an Ethic of Care*. New York: Routledge.

Tronto, J.T. 2013. *Caring Democracy: Markets, Equality and Justice*. New York and London: New York University Press.

Van Binsbergen, W.M.J. 2001. Ubuntu and the Globalization of Southern African Thought and Society. *Quest: An African Journal of Philosophy* 15 (1/2): 53–89.

Van der Velde, M., P. Jansen, and N. Anderson. 2004. *Guide to Management Research Methods*. Malden: Blackwell.

Waghid, Y., and P. Smeyers. 2012. Reconsidering Ubuntu: On the Educational Potential of a Particular Ethic of Care. *Educational Philosophy and Theory* 44 (s2): 6–20.

White, H. 2002. Combining Qualitative and Quantitative Approaches in Poverty Analysis. *World Development* 30 (3): 511–522.

Whyte, K.O., and C. Cuomo. 2016, April. Ethics of Caring in Environmental Ethics: Indigenous and Feminist Philosophies. In *The Oxford Handbook of Environmental Ethics*, edited by Stephen M. Gardiner and Allen Thompson. https://doi.org/10.1093/oxfordhb/9780199941339.013.22.

Wong, W.I., V. Pasterski, P.C. Hindmarsh, M.E. Geffner, and M. Hines. 2012. Are There Parental Socialization Effects on the Sex-Typed Behavior of Individuals with Congenital Adrenal Hyperplasia? *Archives of Sexual Behavior* 42: 381–391. Published Online 21 November 2011. https://doi.org/10.1007/s10508-012-9997-4.

Yin, R.K. 2003. *Case Study Research: Design and Methods. 3rd Edition, Applied Social Research Methods Series*, Vol. 5. Thousand Oaks, London, and New Delhi: Sage.

CHAPTER 5

Wartime Care Work Arrangements and Provision in Darfur Case

5.1 The Status of African Women in Pre-conflict Situation

Most regions in Africa that have experienced or are experiencing armed conflict are still to attain the level of peace and stability of Darfur. The status of women reflects the meaningful properties of their social reality. Africa is probably the most culturally, ethnically, and religiously diverse continent in the world (Appiah et al. 2018). Sudan is one of the most ethnically diverse countries in Africa, with nineteen major linguistic groups and over 600 sub-groups. The Sudanese society as do many other African societies have traditions and cultures that enforce gendered roles, with distinct male and female social roles and responsibilities. Women are assigned "feminine duties". This is informed by gender norms and stereotypes held against the capabilities of women. Public affairs and decision-making for the whole community are primarily the responsibilities of men, while women are subjected to private, mostly family, affairs. The resistance men put up against taking up care and domestic tasks is fuelled by deeply held gender norms, which end up creating social barriers (Peacock 2003). In Sudan, it is considered a taboo by culture for adult males to perform "female activities" such as housekeeping chores, caregiving, etc (Ibnouf 2009).

There are similarities in the roles held by women in Darfur in pre-conflict and in the roles held by women in other African regions.

F. O. Ibnouf, *War-Time Care Work and Peacebuilding in Africa*, Gender, Development and Social Change,
https://doi.org/10.1007/978-3-030-26195-5_5

African, as well as Darfurian tribes are structured on the basis of patriarchal culture and ethnicity. These tribes regard women as inferior to men, and abuse their rights. Patriarchy has been defined as a gendered power system, networks of social, political, and economic relationships through which men dominate and control female labour, reproduction, and sexuality as well as define women's status, privileges, and rights in a society (Kalabamu 2006: 237). Care is a key feminist concern because its arrangement and provision remain so strictly gendered that it defines what men and women can do (Himmelweit and Plomien 2014: 446). In the African culture, it is but normal and expected of the woman to be well aware of her care and domestic work responsibilities. The perception that "a carer is a woman" is passed on from generation to generation. In periods prior to conflict, African women are engaged in subsistence agricultural production (mostly unpaid work), alongside care work and domestic activities. The state merely recognizes the value of unpaid care work. African governments have taken an ambiguous position on the issue of unpaid care work. Most African policies tend to bestow a privilege upon traditional family structures of care provision (Moussié and Alfers 2016). McCarthy (2018) posits that, worldwide, women and girls perform up to 80% of domestic work as shown by the World Bank records (2011) unpaid care work performed by women in Africa is the most challenging worldwide. Unfortunately, these activities are not labelled as "economically active employment" in national accounts, though they are essential for the well-being of households. Since the home is not generally regarded as a workplace, tasks performed at home are not regarded as "real work" (Kynaston 1996: 224).

In a traditional African society, men/boys are not expected to perform care work duties as women/girls. Mothers internalize the "ideal womanhood" belief in girls that their purpose is to take care of the basic family affairs. Moral values and cultural norms which are inculcated into this young generation become guiding principles throughout their lives. Thus, they become inherently submissive to their husbands, endure miserable marriages, and are inclined to satisfying basic family needs—even in complex situations like wartime and its aftermath. To sum up, womanhood is associated with caregiving. However, womanhood is perceived disreputably in these patriarchal societies as in Darfur. Psychologists and sociologists have proven that social forces rather than anatomy shape gender everywhere, yet, girls grow up considering domestic responsibilities to be their primary goal (Ramaswamy 2005). The perception that a woman is the ideal caregiver is a result of patriarchal power structures. Thus, customs define the responsibilities and expectations attached to "women's work", which in turn shape the womanhood philosophy. This philosophy is not unique to the African continent, but rather it is worldwide. Carol Gilligan's (1982) *In a Different Voice* argues that women evaluate themselves according to their ability to care. It is critical to evaluate the caring abilities of women with respect to their particular cultures. When discussing women, care often pop up because women shoulder the majority of the world's care work burden, and their moral agency tends to be characterized by practices of care towards particular others (Robinson 2011). To make this claim is not to make a claim about women's essential nature but about the feminization of care in most societies around the world (ibid.).

A good number of studies carried out in Africa affirm that women and men are placed in different socio-economic contexts with gendered roles defined by culture. This renders women more liable to perform unpaid care work than men (see for example, Berry 2018). In most African cultures, social stereotypes associate masculinity with authority, and differentiates between a "man's work" and a "woman's work". These stereotypes become social norms in social institutions, though they may not be individually approved of (Elson 1999: 611). The predominance of women in care work is largely due to a social construct determined by patriarchal traditions and values (Hirway 2015). Even though the division of labour is tailored by the local population, it tends to be viewed by the members of that society as inevitable and natural (Eagly and Wood 2012: 466). Thus, women take up roles that make up the female gender roles (ibid.: 467). The uneven distribution of unpaid work across gender forms the bases of gender inequality (Hirway 2015). In order to preserve traditions and customs, African women occupy roles in society handed down from mother to daughter, which stereotype them as inferior. There are more cross-cultural similarities in the African traditional gender legacies than differences, like gendered work, unequal access to economic opportunities such as less access to productive resources or to basic education and health services by women (Ibnouf and Manyungwa 2019). African women usually play a vital role in actualizing gendered care work, ensuring the perpetuation of these roles. This gendered labour negatively impacts the prospects of girls as some drop out of school to assist in care activities (Marphatia and Moussié 2013). Change can be resisted (consciously or unconsciously) by society and even by women because it is viewed by some as antithetical to their societal values and cultural beliefs. Women are not a homogenous group although they share the same experiences within the society. Some women accept the gender stereotypes and internalize these beliefs as invaluable cultural values in their own self concepts. These beliefs are partly attributed to the limited understanding of religion or the erroneous application of certain rules. Thus, these stereotypes reflect and shape culture and have remained constant for generations. Experiences of gender stereotypes are being reinforced as a result of armed conflict. Parpart (2017: 54) states that division of labour by gender in conflict zones follows the traditional assumptions of attaching women, girls, and femininity to care work, and men/masculinity to protection and leadership. Embedded norms and stereotypes shape everyday behaviours and decision-making, ranging from the decision of whether to educate daughters or sons when money is scarce, or to promote a man or a woman into a managerial position (Seguino 2011: 1308). Despite the fact that some people may want to get rid of these stereotypes, cultures are always changing. Change, during and after armed conflict in particular, influences the balance of power and gender stereotypes.

In Africa, unpaid private and paid public care work is an issue. Unpaid private care work is usually considered to be of lesser importance than paid public care work. Consequently, women as caregivers are invisible to the state, their rights and well-being overlooked. The notion that men "naturally" belong to the public and civic sphere and women to the private sphere of the family have shaped institutional structures for many centuries and have constituted a major stumbling block to achieving gender equity (Bakari and Leach 2007: 90). Undoubtedly, armed conflicts negatively affect women, but may positively contribute to uplifting their reputation by changing gender roles, assigning women to "men's work". Nonetheless, patriarchal ideologies are maintained as Bouta et al. (2005) mention that while changes in gender roles often do take place, the ideological basis underpinning gender relations may remain largely unchanged. Cerrato and Cifre (2018) cited that from a cultural and discursive perspective, gender ideology, defined as beliefs and values maintained about what are right for men and women, determines the patterns by which a particular society judges or evaluates the proper. Women have carried these common patriarchal traditions for ages in pre- and post-conflict eras, and they are passed from one generation to another. The continued existence of this ideology—unequal involvement in care work and household chores—will contribute to wide gaps between men and women (gender inequality), if left unaddressed. Despite their role as caregivers, women in pre-conflict and during wartime still face unfathomable suffering. Their contribution to society as caregivers is ignored in economic data. Many women face sexual and physical violence, and harmful traditional practices. Some scholars highlight the interplay between culture and the interpretation of violence against women, rendering it heroic, justified, reasonable, or at least acceptable (Merry 2009).

In Africa, most women work in the informal sector as compared to men—89.7% for women in comparison to 82.7% for men, and for non-agricultural employment, 78.6% for women and 67.7% for men (ILO 2018). Care work preoccupies women, depriving them from taking up better paid jobs in the formal sector. Thus, they are trapped in casual or informal and low-income work. The pressure of trying to balance work and childcare can lead women to take up jobs of a lower status, often in the informal sector (Samman et al. 2016). Africa is characterized by more female participants in the informal sector of the economy without access to social protection (Moussié and Alfers 2016). Informality has a harmful effect on workers' rights, including fundamental principles and rights at work, social protection, decent working conditions, and the rule of law (ILO 2018). The burden borne by women and girls because they put in more hours in care work and household chores than the opposite sex reduces the time available for education and thus chances of acquiring better jobs.

5.2 The Lived Experiences of Caregivers During Wartime

In Darfur, women contribute considerably to the survival and the well-being of their families through performing daily unpaid care activities during and after armed conflict. The fulfilment of these activities entails physical, emotional, and social efforts, alongside invaluable time put in. There is a distinction between care as ethic and care as practice. Care as ethic is normative and describe what good care looks like, while care as practice ultimately focuses on caring and embodies physical and emotional work (Raghuram 2016). Time is a critical factor and can be considered an important resource during wartime. Caregiving is an important part of the lives of women, as affirmed in the focus groups' conceptualization of womanhood and care work. Womanhood is associated with caregiving and the responsibilities of ensuring the well-being of the family. The role of women as caregivers is apparent during conflict, as they endure enormous challenges. Wartime care work arrangements are definitely more arduous than in normal/peacetime. The caregivers in wartime have limited resources with little or no support from the state and/or NGOs. Consequently, almost the entire burden of care work and daily household activities are shouldered by women. The interviewees made it obvious that in wartime, they face serious time constraints. They tend to give back to society far more than they take, and they use care work to give new life and energy to Darfur.

Caregivers' response to the realities of the situation is consistent with the ability of women to cope in wartime and to rebuild their lives in the aftermath of war. The interviews and group discussions carried out in Darfur indicates that women during wartime sacrifice everything in order to sustain their families, irrespective of how terrified, scared, upset, and sad they may be. They demonstrated impregnable commitments to fulfilling the care needs of their loved ones, despite of how arduous it might be. Here, wartime care arrangements are time-consuming and demands prompt responses, often requiring the performance of physical activities alongside psychological and emotional support. Care work takes up a great deal of the time available to women, whether or not they are job holders (Samman et al. 2016). The ethics of care refers to a moral framework characterized by an ontological commitment to relationality and care as the basis of human well-being (Robinson 2011).

Care and ethics are influenced by culture, traditions, indigenous norms, and religion. Wartime care work is complex and quite different from care work in peacetime. As a moral duty, women are consumed by care activities in order to protect and sustain the lives of their children and family members, among others, even in the most dangerous circumstances. "*Whenever* a *need for care arises, it is much harder to choose not to offer help*", added the female interviewees. *At that moment, no one ever doubts or questions their abilities to arrange and provide care.* We perform *care work without hesitation. During wartime, we feel responsible for caring for anyone not on the basis of kinship or personal relations. We attend to needs so long as they adhere with our values and customs, even though sometimes we may be putting ourselves at risk.* They went on steadfastly that—*Our duty to care for our family and community is not a set of enforced rules but rather of ethical codes*. The responsibility to provide care during wartime is a moral one. What matters most at that moment is figuring out the actions to undertake in order to save a life or to heal a pain. Care ethics refers to approaches to moral life and the community that are grounded in virtues, practices, and knowledge associated with appropriate caring and caretaking of the self and others (Whyte and Cuomo 2016).

Having cultural and religious values, moral beliefs, patience, empathy, sympathy, confidence, and altruism qualify women as caregivers during and after conflict. The interviewees emphasized that—*Caring is a moral obligation. During wartime I cannot turn away from an injured person in need of help. We are providing not only physical support but also concern and love*. The experiences of women coupled with their everyday struggles during wartime, ultimately compel them to focus on satisfying the needs of others above theirs. *Caregiving is enmeshed in our values and beliefs, which sometimes leaves us neglecting the satisfaction of our own needs*—the women explain. It is clear that it is mainly women who put the attainment of their life objectives second to the obligations associated with carrying out unpaid tasks in the home and community (Domínguez-Serrano 2012).

While the scope and purpose of this study does not aim to use time-use surveys, however time is of the utmost importance to caregivers during wartime. Wartime care work entails long and often unrecognized hours on arduous tasks that fall primarily onto women. The time spent on care is determined by the number of those in need of care and the complexity of the care work to be performed. Time is the key determinant in wartime, every minute counts. When asked about how much time they spend on caring, the women responded—*24 hours a day, you take on more work to respond to arising urgent needs. There is no time to rest, no sleep in almost every seemingly endless night. We are the first on scene to respond. It is an extremely difficult task, but still we work tirelessly in every way for the survival of our children and families. We call on God to strengthen us and grant us patience*. An interviewee proceeds—*I would rather face any kind of pain than the look on my parent's and children's faces when they go hungry*. Some of the tasks cannot be disentangled from each other and are often performed simultaneously (for example, cooking while supervising a child). These tasks are physically exhausting for caregivers.

In wartime, women carry on care work activities under life threatening conditions and adversities with physical, psychological, and social repercussions. The interviewees share some of the challenging experiences they encountered in the arrangement and provision of care work. These stories are essential to understanding the daily struggles for survival in the cyclical nature of conflicts. *We do feel exhausted, fatigued and confused with our current predicaments and tend to blame external factors*—they say—*but we need to be empowered from within to pull through. We make difficult decisions in certain circumstances either to be the masters of our own fate by responding with kindness and care or to be the victims.* They further narrate that *we are victims of a war not of our making, a predicament beyond our control, but staying a victim is a choice, one that should never be accepted as inevitable and inescapable. War renders its victims vulnerable e.g. to trauma, fortunately most of the horrific experiences fade out with time. Our parents and in laws were depressed, experienced sleeping and behavioural disorders while our children developed poor appetites for food and frequent night time urinations.* During wartime, victims suffer from the absence of basic need services because the providers (humanitarian organizations and NGOs) are restrained by insecurities from gaining access to the needy. The women do mention that some cases require the services of health care professionals, who unfortunately are never available. The caregivers thus resort to natural remedies. *We continue caring for the sick and injured family members with the use of traditional remedies*—says the women. *We are progressing peacefully in life.*

Conflict destroys the means to livelihood (land, homesteads, productive trees, and wells) and basic care infrastructures. The interviewees were in agreement that war experiences do result in traumatic memories. Due to the extensive effects it has on people's lives as well as the massive social changes that ensue, war is one of those special phenomena that leave strong memories in the minds of those experiencing it (Jamshidiha and Hamidi 2007 cited in Rahimaghaee et al. 2016). The interview rooms were filled with pain and sorrow as these women described the loss of their homes, farmlands, and livestock that took them years to acquire—*Unforgettable memories of watching our houses and its contents burnt to the ground as we were forced to flee our homelands.*

The primary concern of ethics of care is the value of care in sustaining and nurturing human life.

The sample surveyed indicated that care is provided without question to those in dire need of it in conflict and post-conflict situations.

For women, care work is assumed to complement not only cultural norms and expectations, but also moral and religious obligations. *Caring is an ethical and religious obligation and caring for those who need care the most is a form of worship to God*—affirms the interviewees. *Caring for our family is not something we negotiate with others; it is a daily practice that demands integrity and authenticity. It is the personal commitment that we carry in our hearts.* Ethics are based on accepting others and relating to them.

Wartime care work arrangement requires that women, already involved in complex tasks should protect their dependents at high risk of personal injury and/or other forms of war crimes, as is evident in Darfur. *We suppress our pain and challenge our predicament rather than embracing it. We experience increasing needs for care services. We have no choice but to care but to care for the many because things are just that bad. It is not easy.*

As aforementioned, women face many challenges resulting from armed conflict. It takes a lot be a caregiver during conflict as compared to peacetimes. Experiences women undergo during these dire periods imbue them with additional knowledge that improves their caregiving skills. One of the women interviewed expresses—*If it were not for women, the suffering of many, especially the children, elderly, sick, wounded and disabled, would have worsen as the conflict went on.* Despite the challenges, Khadija, aged 32 and a widow with 5 children states—*Caregiving is love.* Others add—*In such dire circumstances, being a caregiver means that you are responsible for the continuous survival and wellbeing of your family. What makes us strong is our knowledge of how to survive difficult times. What makes care work special is because it is voluntary and it ensures the prospects of our future generation; our children.* Thus, women as caregivers meet the requirements.

War delivers the hidden talents and brings out the best in these women. In wartime, care works are diverse and can include predicaments that need medicinal drugs and the services of a professional healthcare worker. The women substituted medicinal drugs for natural remedies and professional healthcare workers for themselves. They treated wounds by applying crushed garlic gloves or lemon powder on them. They served as midwifes by drawing inspiration from traditional childbearing practices. They also buried the dead. Consequently, in post-conflict, some of these women perfected these skills through formal education and became professional midwives.

In war, women make the most of the limited resources to make ends meet. They explore every available option that can improve their livelihood, especially that which increases their food supply. This begs the question: In conflict, through what means do women with very little incomes, food, and other livelihood resources nourish their families? Life is reduced to mere existence, and unsuitable foods like wild foods and insects become vital for survival. In conflict zones, people eat insects such as termites and locusts out of necessity, usually collected by women (see for example, Al-Safi 2007). The African mourning dove (*Streptopelia Decipiens*) and red-billed quelea (*Quelea Quelea*) have been identified as sources of emergency food when food is scarce in areas affected by conflict in Sudan (Mirghani 2007). Quelea is a common food in most areas in Africa experiencing conflict; these birds may be smoked or sundried for preservation (Elliott et al. 2014).

Insecurity is of the biggest concern during war. Care work and domestic activities are time-consuming both in war and peace times. These activities can wear out caregivers physically, socially, and psychologically. They perform healthcare tasks that are normally performed by healthcare professionals. Despite how tough it already is for a normal person; some women have kids and family members with disability requiring special needs. They do however make sure these needs are satisfied optimally.

In post-conflict, the survivors in general have needs, and the rape victims or mothers with children as a result of rape need special care. Some of the experiences these women went through are horrific and it is unbelievable that they still found the courage and means to provide care. Rape is a particularly sensitive topic to discuss in any context, yet some of the rape victims still endured the interview. Among them was a young woman with three legitimate children, and a fourth child born of rape. Eyes filled with tears; she exclaims—*it is hard to love someone that ignites painful memories each time you take a look at them*. She pauses for a while and continues—*I love and care for him, because he's my son, but he is also the son of my enemy, the man who killed my husband*. Rape can result to serious physical, as well as mental or psychological problems, and even death. Some of the victims described the feeling as—*Becoming pregnant as a consequence of rape, coerced, or incapacitated from tending to your children is a terrible feeling*. In Darfur and in most conflict zones in Africa, there are no mechanisms in place to investigate rape, thus the perpetrators are exempted from punishment.

Being the primary caregivers, women bear the weight of care work irrespective of the state they are in. The sample surveyed for this study also comprises of pregnant women and women with newborns. The workloads on these women have serious health repercussions. Miscarriages are a common phenomenon affecting these women as they carry on arduous care work activities without adequate rest during wartime and in the aftermath of war. To these women, the fulfilment of care work is of much importance than their personal well-being. They perform caregiving activities under difficult circumstances while managing their personal traumatic experiences such as rape or other forms of assault, or the loss of a loved one. They are also exposed to injury and other war-related crimes. Despite all these challenges, women as caregivers get a great deal of satisfaction and self-fulfilment from what they do.

The emotional element of caring cannot be static; it cannot be replaced by any means. Eyben (2012) points out that the emotional element, unlike housework, cannot be fully replaced by labour-saving technology. During wartime, women as caregivers/providers work out of love, altruism, sheer sympathy, and empathy for their families or others. As revealed by the interviewed women, they feel complete and fulfilled when they care for those who need their assistance; for their own family and any others. For them, caring for a person irrespective of the relation you have with him/her is motivated by their religious beliefs and respect for cultural values. They expect nothing in return, just a show of gratitude.

Social networks are the bases of survival and protection in difficult times. In wartime, these networks are broken down resulting in compounding workloads on women as caregivers. The women's group in IDPs camps discusses the dynamics of conflicts, its impacts and consequences on care work, and how it shapes the relationships established between individuals and groups in the process of building social networks in the IDPs camps. The demographic composition of a society shifts dramatically in and after conflict and women endure a concomitant increase in roles and work load—household headship, decision-makers, expansion of their roles into the public affairs, etc.

Culture is crucial to understanding and responding to the effects of conflict. Whatever the disputes, feminist research is quite unanimous about the overall logic of present gender systems: it is male domination (Rantalaiho et al. 1997). During war, women become caregivers and providers alike, and at the same time the protectors of their family. It was repeatedly raised in interviews and focus group discussions that—*Now, women are responsible for everything. Despite our family's and community's reliance on us, our burden is yet to be noticed or valued.* Almost all participants agreed that care work arrangements had been a tedious and very stressful activity, but a rewarding one as it safeguarded their loved ones and community at large. One of the interviewees lamented—*what a pity, hard unpaid care work remains in obscurity, but it will be illuminated and valued one day.* The ethics of care focuses on giving a voice to the voiceless. Many of the women interviewed for this study revealed that their participation enlightened them on the state they are in, and hopes this study becomes a medium for making their voices and opinions heard—*There is hope for our empowerment because after the war, we have woken up from a very deep slumber. We will continue to advocate for equal redistribution of care work responsibilities so that we, both young and old, and like men can begin to live well by paying more attention to our personal needs. We need to transmit proper legacies to our children, who in turn will do the same to their own children.*

The topic as to whether women possess relevant knowledge and ideas on the manner peacebuilding should be carried out was raised during interviews and focus group discussions. *It is a pity that our stories as care workers during and after do not count as an important source of information for policymaking*—*they responded. We do not rely on others to take care of our families during war and we definitely do not need them to build peace on our behalf.* They insist on knowing what is best for them. Their perspectives and priorities vary considerably from those of their spokespersons. *All our efforts invested in life saving implies we are skilful at reconstruction. We know what is required and should be entrusted with leading roles in peace building. Rather, we are substituted with experts who are clueless of the realities of the conflict we lived.* Peace building should be carried out pragmatically. The women who with little or nothing, pragmatically endured the harsh conditions of conflict are best suited to ensure this. They supported the burden of providing care work for the survival and protection of their families.

What lessons can be drawn from the lived experiences of care workers in conflict? A qualitative analysis of the unstructured interviews and focus group discussions revealed in depth the lived experiences of wartime care work arrangements and the perceptions of conflict by women as caregivers. The female participants for this study held unaccustomed socio-economic and cultural statuses similar to those of women in the

IDPs camps. The challenges they faced and how they overcame them shaped their manner of care work provision. Wartime unpaid care work is time-consuming, physically and emotionally demanding. Daly and Lewis (2000: 285) define care as the activities and relations involved in meeting the physical and emotional requirements of the dependent adults and children, the normative, economic, and social frameworks within which these are assigned and carried out. Thus, care work provision by women during wartime means they are major actors in sustaining life. With limited resources (money, basic need services, relief aid packages), the absence of social networks, rampant human rights violations, unjust patriarchal systems and cultural beliefs, alongside other challenges of armed conflict facing women, they work round-the-clock as caregivers for their immediate and extended families, and for their community as a whole. Many feminist scholars are concerned with the bulk of care work, entailing long and often undervalued hours of performing arduous tasks that fall primarily on women (Marphatia and Moussié 2013). However, the role women play in wartime is deemed to be of utmost importance by their male counterparts. *Now and during wartime, without women we are nothing*—they admitted during the focus group discussions. The rest of the participants for this study strongly support this fact. Care work arrangements and provisions had been vital for the survival and well-being of their families and community. Unpaid care work is both an important aspect of economic activities and an indispensable factor contributing to the well-being of individuals, their families, and societies (Stiglitz et al. 2007) and to the peace. It will be laudable element of improving peacebuilding processes if taken into consideration.

5.3 Care Work in Post-conflict Situation: Changing or Still the Same

The predicaments of women in war zones are bad, and tend to worsen as they become IDPs. They are still preoccupied with the provision of numerous care work activities. Despite the repressive societal and cultural norms against women's self-development, they are responsible for almost everything. In addition to being caregivers, they are also breadwinners for their families. This is because their male counterparts, normally the head of the family and breadwinner, are either in the battle fields, dead, captured, trapped, incapacitated, etc., forcing women to replace them in the home. Men are the primary targets in war, forcing them to migrate to different locations and lower paying jobs or to wholly rely on their women for the upkeep of the household. El-Bushra and Sahl (2005) comment that in Sudan, displacements into towns exposed women to the possibilities of building networks and acquiring new skills, while the men remained unable to be the breadwinners due to loss of cattle and land. The dichotomy between women as primary caregivers and men as primary breadwinners needs to be squashed (Marphatia and Moussié 2013).

The adage *experience is the best teacher* best explains the improvement in the problem-solving skills of women in conflict zones. They face numerous onerous obstacles and challenges in the arrangement and provision of care work during and in the aftermath of war, and are able to overcome them by their growing experience. In post-conflict, the women's focus groups discussed what is next in their agenda—*We have no other choice but to start rebuilding our lives all over again. We still continue to care for those in need of our help, not just our family members but for all the others; orphans, the elderly* etc. *Putting a smile on their faces means the world to us. To us, it is the most rewarding feeling in this life.* Many of them go through certain adversities in rebuilding their lives. However, almost all of the women interviewed agreed that care work is essential as it continuously lessen the suffering and losses during and after the conflict.

Care work in wartime is more complex and arduous than in the absence of war. Also, living in IDPs camps comes with its own new challenges to caregivers. *We adapt the manner in which we provide care to the changes in the post-conflict settings*—the female participants explain. *As caregivers, we keep moving forward, opening new doors and doing new things. Care work keeps leading us down new paths for the benefit of our families and community.* Caregivers are the cornerstones in rebuilding a pragmatic and peaceful community after conflict.

In the post conflict in Darfur, displaced women take care of larger numbers in the family because they are now the sole providers, while enduring post-traumatic stresses related to the conflict. They explain—*Keeping our feet firmly on the ground is not easy and is so unappreciated.* One continues—*I have seven children, my old parents and four orphans to take care of. With my husband dead, I am their sole provider and supporter. Fortunately for me I have a decent paying job. I cannot imagine what it would have be like for them without me.*

Livelihoods of the post-conflict communities can be characterized as "livelihoods at risk". Most people have no access to their pre-conflict livelihoods, which are based on a combination of farming, herding, trade, and seasonal labour migration (Buchanan-Smith and Jaspars 2007). The roles of rural women are flexible, responding to evolving circumstances. Thus, gendered labour is changing accordingly with women taking up breadwinner responsibilities formally occupied by men in wartime and post-war periods. This study indicated that women are faced with greater responsibilities as most of them have to work harder to secure food for their family single-handed. Subsistence or survival-based activities form yet another type of unpaid work performed predominately by women that is socially undervalued and not recorded in economic accounts of work (Hobbs and Rice 2018: 100). Such activities may include care work, rearing of small animals, domestic activities, and food processing. Some of the domestic activities include fetching water and firewood. Water is a basic necessity in life and firewood is the main source of cooking fuel. The other major concern is the time and effort spent on these activities. Women have to walk for miles and spend hours of day light fetching water and firewood. These hours and efforts could have been spent on more productive and self-improving activities. These hours may double or even triple during the dry season.

In Darfur, the displaced women optimally utilize the limited resources at their disposal for care work arrangement and provision, and for domestic activities. These activities are divided into tasks such as food preparation which includes fetching water and firewood, and others. Traditional foods provide optimum solutions to hunger, given the availability of raw materials (Dirar 1993). Women in most African countries use a diverse number of simple and traditional processing techniques to make a variety of traditional food products. Traditional food processing techniques are simple and low-cost and aim to increase the shelf life of the food products (Ibnouf 2012). So, processed foods kept at room temperature can last for a long period without getting spoilt and are a good source of nourishment when fresh produce is scarce (ibid.). There is no electricity in IDP camps. The indigenous foods have been continued to be the foods for survival during wartime and in IDP's situations. Traditional food processing techniques (fermentation, salting, smoking, drying, etc.) are simple to perform, cheap to employ, and increase the shelf life of the produce. Wild undomesticated foods such as kawal *(Cassia obtusifolia)*, green leafy vegetable (*Sonchus* sp.), and some inedible wild foods at their current states are processed by women into conventional food products like makhait (*Boscia senegalensis*). A favourite choice to the meat substitute is kawal (see Fig. 5.1). Kawal is one of the most popular dishes in western Sudan and is derived from the two-week long fermentation of the pounded green leaves of the kawal (*Cassia obtusifolia*). Edible insects, for example, the desert locust (*Schistocerca gregaria*) and birds, for example, the red-billed quelea (*Quelea quelea*) are used as emergency foods during and in the aftermath of war. International aid programs so far are unable to solve the problem of food insecurity in and out of war.

Another important issue that was brought up during the group discussions was gendered labour. Displaced women are considered to be the pillars of the family in providing care services necessary for sustenance and well-being. This entails less and less time for paid work. However, in post-conflict, they are entering the job market in increasing numbers. This challenges the dichotomy between men as breadwinners and

Fig. 5.1 Women make traditional for survival (kawal as meat substitute) (This photo was taken by the research assistant Abd-Alrahman Ibrahim, 2016)

women as homemakers. The women can now earn their own income, rendering them independent and decision makers. Women as caregivers, in the absence of men as breadwinners and of support social systems, have no choice but to accept informal low-paying jobs. Women are more likely to have their employment jeopardized by their performance of caring activities than men (Schofield et al. 1998). Although they work hard for less pay in the informal sector, in bad working conditions with no social protections, these jobs are flexible and can be adjusted to make room for their fulfilment of care work duties, thus creating a balance between paid and unpaid work. One of the interviewees stated—*You are irreplaceable in your family, but you can be replaced on a job, isn't it?* Therefore, women place caregiving for their families first, although it may jeopardize their employment. The point is, work flexibility is of utmost importance for most women as caregivers. Public policy fails in ensuring this aspect—not enough is being done to support families in balancing the demands of work and childcare (Samman et al. 2016). Work flexibility in the informal sector is important to caregivers/providers because they tend to have a balanced lifestyle—balancing work and caregiving.

Educated women in Darfur occupy subordinate jobs with less pay (e.g. secretaries, clerks, and the likes) that provide support services to their male superiors. This hierarchical structure is typical of and originates from the common family structure where wives are homemakers and husbands are decision makers. Many of the women entering the job market are assigned to jobs considered socially appropriate for women, thus leading to the segregation of gender by occupation (Folbre and Nelson 2000). They make up most of the workforce in the informal sector as can be seen in Fig. 5.3, which shows that most of the women interviewed work at the brick baking kilns near El-Fashier, the capital city of Darfur to the North. They endure terrible working conditions, longer hours of work, and are poorly compensated. Thus, they are exploited by their bosses (mostly men), their rights abused, and they tend to lose their dignity. Mothers have to take their children to work with them, some with swathed infants (refer to Fig. 5.2). One of the women with three kids aged one, three, and five narrated—*Brick making demands a lot of physical strength, but it fits my schedule because I can bring my little children with me to work. They are not yet in school and I have no one else to take care of them in my absence, so I bring them to work with me every day.* This routine gets the job done while at the same time offering care

Fig. 5.2 Displaced women are working in brick baking kilns (This photo was taken by the author, North Darfur State, 2016)

services to their kids. Though the job has ill-health repercussions, it is a critical constituent for the survival of their families. Another woman continues—*it is not a glamorous job, but it is something I am very proud of because I earn enough money to cover for my family's daily needs and my kids' school fees.* Some of them reported that their husbands are reluctant to take on jobs, irrespective of its nature. During the interviews, women were reluctant to reveal the truth about their unpleasant working conditions. In order to secure their jobs, they protect their abusive bosses, perpetuating the violations of their rights as humans. *We are faced with no other option but to accept our jobs. The money we make is used for feeding, shelter, medicine, schooling* etc. *It is our life support.* Paid and unpaid works are often criss-crosses. Some women have to leave their jobs to care for the needy. The number of girls per family willing and able to perform caregiving duties determines the number of hours their mothers put into their jobs and the decision they make as to whether or not to be part of the labour force.

One of every three female interviewees is a widow, divorced, or separated from their husbands because they are missing or disappeared. As a consequence, the women become the head of the household as well as care providers. They face serious time constraints and may have to work for fewer hours in the formal sector or choose poorly paid jobs in the informal sector where their schedule can be easily adjusted to suit their routine. *It is very stressful to be the family's caregiver and also work outside the house to earn money. I have to pay for food and schooling. I cannot*

Fig. 5.3 IDP women grassroots organizations and illiteracy classes (This photo was taken by the research assistant Dr. Mohamed Teabin, 2016)

afford to take time off—they say. Brimblecombe et al. (2018) postulate the the intensity of caregiving is a significant factor in determining whether carers get and maintain a job. An interviewee commented—*I am usually the first in the family to get out of bed and the last to go to bed. Only God knows how I'm able to manage between paid work and domestic duties. I wake up before daybreak to perform my household chores (mostly fetching water and firewood, and cooking) before going to work at sunrise. Some chores I perform on my return from work.*

Children have the right to education. Many displaced girls in post-conflict are un-enrolled in school because they are preoccupied with care work for their siblings when their mothers are dead or incapacitated as a result of war. The rights of these girls are protected by the Convention on the Rights of the Child (CRC), including the right to education. However, implementation takes political will, resources, and administrative capacity. A girl, aged 16 narrates her story—*I lost both parents, two of my brothers and my eldest sister to the war. I became the sole provider for my family at the age of 14. Hence the satisfaction of all the needs of my family became my responsibility.* She paused and took a deep breath before going on *I have no time to go to school.* To female family heads in post-war, very little time is available for rest, formal education, professional training, and thus for being part of the labour force (Blackden and Wodon 2006; Hirway 2015).

After war, physical injuries are visible to the eye but the psychological injuries are psychogenic. Some of the participants feel degraded and has low self-esteem, with distorted identities. The severity of psychological injuries is fully understood only when the victims open up. Nevertheless, psychosocial care is insufficient in post-conflict. Women as caregivers also need care. There are still limited government agencies and NGOs that are specialized in catering for victims of posttraumatic stress. Only the most basic social services are provided by the state in IDPs camps, and these services are inadequate. Poorly executed Water, Sanitation, and Hygiene (WASH) and housing programs lead to the metastasis of influenza and diarrhoea among children in IDPs camps. *Watching your child suffer is a painful experience*—the women exclaimed. The lack of basic infrastructures and public services renders the already disproportionate share of unpaid care work borne by women more arduous, which impinges on their capacity to earn an income and accrue savings, and also has negative impacts on their health and well-being (Moussié and Alfers 2016).

The women in group discussions were seriously bothered by the unequal responsibilities of care work borne between them and men. The women, as do Gasper et al. (2008) affirm that care facilitates the achievement of the most basic goals in life (survival, well-being, and self-development). In wartime, public caregiving services are non-existent. If not for these women, the misery and wretchedness of the needy, especially the children, elderly, and disabled, would have been intolerable. The women did mention that—*The problems of internal displacements cannot be overcome with food aids from external donors only.* Without a change in social attitudes towards care work responsibilities, women will continue to carry most of its burden. While civil war imposes tremendous burdens on women, it often contributes to the redefinition of their traditional roles and the reconfiguration of existing gender relations in the society (Kumar 2001).

In pitiful situations are women treated as outcasts because they were sexually violated during war. This stigmatization extends to their children born of rape. These women and their children fend for themselves. Being raped can have lifelong terrible consequences for girls and women, which worsen when they give birth as a product of the sexual assault (Atim et al. 2018).

The question then that comes to mind is whether the caregivers consider their caregiving experiences during and after war to be terrible or wonderful. The caregivers interviewed seemed to relate more to the positive impacts of care work to the survival of their families rather than the horrors they experienced in performing care work. They reported having wonderful caregiving experiences because their work sustained their families and communities. They took it upon themselves as a moral obligation to protect their family members and ensure that they have a life purpose, and as a duty to incite togetherness and cooperation in their communities and the IDPs camps. They came through and thus feel self-fulfilled, satisfied, appreciated, and proud. The caregivers remain contented even as care needs increase. Sooner or later, caregivers are admitted to be pivotal for survival, attracting more and more dependents (Fauziana et al. 2018). The positive aspect of caregiving has been defined as the gains or satisfactory feelings resulting from the caregiving experience (Abdollahpour et al. 2018).

The lessons drawn from the lived experiences of caregivers are essential for peacebuilding. These women are resilient. They fulfil their duties no matter what happens. Most of them are the breadwinners and the caregivers of the family. They are exhausted by onerous work for they cannot afford babysitters and/or time-saving technological appliances, for example, gas stoves. Even in the IDPs camps, access to basic care services is not easy. The longer they stay displaced, the harder it becomes. Being occupied with unpaid care work can deprive women from being a part of the workforce, or force them to work part-time, in low status, lower paid positions (McCarthy 2018: 340). The tough unpaid care work women provide to their dependents and other community members as IDPs are services that the State is supposed to be partly responsible for providing. Although the care work activities become arduous overtime in post-conflict, many of the interviewed women believe that care work added value to their lives.

5.4 Care Solidarity

At the very least, the caregiver's model demonstrates how to build togetherness in service of the entire community with limited resources. The caregivers admitted to rendering care services as a form of solidarity. Sevenhuijzen suggested that care solidarity emphasizes the notions of attentiveness, responsiveness, and responsibility to all sort of situations in which care is required by human beings (Sevenhuijzen 1998 cited in Gasper and Truong 2008).

The shared experiences of war victims bind them together. The IDPs camps host refugees from over forty-six different tribes. These IDPs form intercultural bonds and share care responsibilities for the benefit of all. Women spearhead this solidarity union in a manner of equitable treatment of all individuals for peace and stability. This union creates social networks that facilitate the sharing of resources needed for care provision, survival, and well-being. Africans possess many positive cultural values such as solidarity, tolerance, respect for elders, caring for the needy, sharing, negotiating, discussing, mediating (Idang 2015).

IDPs maintain family and community ties in order to achieve the difficult task of rebuilding their lives from scratch. In the course of interviews and group discussions, the women did mention that in armed conflict, saving lives is their top priority. After the conflict, providing care services to those in need, maintaining personal and communal relationships, rebuilding peaceful communities, and avoiding further social disruptions become the new agendas. *The provision of care work during and after war is something that brings us all together. Unity is strength and living by this philosophy ensures the survival of our young.* This philosophy is typically African, referred to as Ubuntu. Lutz (2009) affirms that people are not individual and independent, but are part of a larger community with relationships and interdependencies.

In IDPs camps, care work creates harmony among its inhabitants. Life here is similar to life in pre-war, a peaceful melting pot. In terms of social security and stability, the women said—*we are opportune to build resilient communities as caregivers. It takes patience and perseverance to achieve such a goal. So, by working together the problems affecting all of us can be easily solved.* They play a crucial role in the process of building peaceful coexistence thus enforcing togetherness, eliminating racial discrimination, and motivating positive relationships among individuals. *We are inspired by our shared experiences when creating the basis for collaboration.* Through care work, they have been able to inspire peaceful intercultural relationships. *Caring creates an ethical culture. It is a moral obligation to care for your family and others in desperate situations. It is about respect, responsibility and trust. These moral values are the key to peaceful coexistence.* A moral disposition and a set of moral sensibilities, issues, and practices that arise from taking seriously the fact that care is a central aspect of human existence refers to an ethic of care (Tronto 1995 cited in Sevenhuijsen et al. 2003). Intermarriages are efficient in mitigating Intertribal conflicts. In the IDPs camps, the displaced women focus on mending the social relationships between opposing tribes during conflict by Interethnic marriages. *Intermarriages eliminate the element of revenge and establish family ties among opposing tribes.* This practice is widespread in IDPs communities for peacekeeping and cohesion among its members. *We always care for, inspire and motivate our people to work together and give their very best.* Moreover, intermarriages may contribute to precluding future conflicts between the tribes. Remenyi (2016) advocates women have significantly impacted peacebuilding processes and outcomes informally at local and grassroots level.

5.5 Violence Against Women: A Call for Concern

Sexual assault and rape[1] are still not well-thought-of in peace talks across Africa. Violence against women, which is becoming prevalent during and after conflict, is perceived to be culturally acceptable and is considered to a heritage, backed by religion and morality. The abuse of the rights of women is worsening in armed conflict. Whether or not they become empowered in post-war from occupying family and societal roles normally reserved for men, they still run the risk being violated. Rape is still a common phenomenon in and around IDP's settlements. Women and girls that leave the camp run a serious risk of being sexually assaulted.

Some of the IDPs poses a threat to women and girls as caregivers. They are at risk of being violated while performing their duties as care workers, such as fetching water and firewood. They must venture outside the safe zone of the camp on a daily basis in order to source these necessities. *We are frequently subjected to rape and abuse when we fetch water and collect firewood. Even when we know the assailants are still there, we go back to the same place again and again to fetch water and firewood. We sell most of the firewood in the nearby market and it is our only source of income. Water is a necessity in life.* One woman added—*I have been beaten several times but I count myself lucky for I do not sustain serious injuries like some of my fellow women do.* One in every three women admitted that they have experienced some sort of violence.

When sexually assaulted, these women are fearful about speaking out for they may be stigmatized. In every group discussion, sexual abuse was depicted as a serious problem for women and girls. The victims are constrained by cultural values to keep quiet about this despicable offence committed against them. Disrespecting cultural norms is very difficult and can be detrimental to one's status in society. However, the women thought—*If we collectively break this code and speak out as victims of sexual violence, it can be a powerful way of stopping such unethical behaviour.* Sexual violence can lead to personality disorder and indignity. The women complained—*it is extremely unfair for women who have been raped to be denied and disowned by their families and community. Finding a sensitive way to approach the issue is a challenge.*

Rape is a complex problem in armed conflict, and responding to it is more complex during and after conflict. It is an uphill battle caring for rape victims. Rape is often used as a weapon of war rather than a crime of opportunity. The purpose of raping the women of an opponent is to get them pregnant (Kinnear 2011; Mani 2011). The aim is that the opposing community should have offspring born of rape, considered "ethically unclean", thus destroying their social and cultural fabric. The victims (mostly girls) are often ostracized from their communities and considered to bring shame. In some cases, children born from rape are scorned by their own mothers (Newbury and Baldwin 2001: 31). These women and girls face a lot of hardship, stigma, and a good number of rape-related health issues. Being alienated by their communities and even in some cases by their families, they face a lot of difficulties reintegrating into the society. The psychic trauma they go through can be unbearable. While abortions cannot alleviate the trauma, they at least offer the victims a fighting chance for their lives and future. The children born of rape carry a stigma, as do their mothers, detrimental to their well-being as human beings.

Apart from the abuse of the rights of women, violence of all sorts has negative consequences to the society. Lessons from the ways in which women counteract violence are essential to reducing the rate of violence. Violence against women can lead to physical and psychological injuries, which influence their ability to carry on care work.

5.6 Carving the Path to Peace—Women Grassroots Organizations

Unpaid care work is invisible and yet to be recognized because time-use data is not yet a regular feature in national statistical systems in many countries, thus care work is not accounted for in economic policies (Hirway 2015). Also, care work is drudgework (ibid.).

Any attempt to build peace requires an understanding of the reality on the ground. In IDPs camps in Darfur, diverse tribes live in peace and harmony, spearheaded by women as caregivers is being involved in collective initiative activities. While these initiative activities may be perceived as a mere extension of care and domestic work, they serve as foundation stones laid by women as caregivers in the informal peace building processes. Women are taking up more active peace roles, especially as initiative organizations, aimed at addressing the abuse of the rights of children, women, and the society, and are also putting in place measures that influence peaceful resolutions of conflicts and that safeguard peace and stability (Rehn and Sirleaf 2009; Shulika and Shulika 2016). Women in IDPs camps are increasingly joining the fight—*We have a role to play in reforming the tradition that places more burden of unpaid care work on our shoulders. Our associations are rooting for change.*

Although both men and women lose their property during war, men are still finding it difficult to become caregivers, and through that peacemakers, unlike women. Internally displaced women in camps are forming grassroots movements to defend their rights and to stand for a peaceful and stronger society. Through shared goals and interests, they work for the benefits of their families and communities. The groups add peacebuilding to the care work agenda. They come up with mutually beneficial solutions to conflict by building social networks that support one another. The formation of these groups creates forums where women can discuss issues surrounding the conflict and advocate for peace (Remenyi 2016). A member from the Abu-Shook IDP camp expresses—*No matter our status in society, if we have a common problem, sharing our experiences and ideas will lead to a step closer to the solution.* These women are fully engaged in informal peacebuilding and solidarity activities. Some of them reported joining the groups for financial support. Although entry is voluntary, group participation became the only major way to engage with others in the IDPs community. These groups empower women as caregivers and as peacemakers. The groups are mostly nameless and are founded by a group of women rather than individually. They offer professional training such as tailoring, artisanship, and even formal education (see Fig. 5.4). Some even pull their resources together to establish and run income generating activities as a group. Very few of these groups have been able to secure funding from donor organizations. Most times than not, they fund themselves. Members of these groups become more powerful, are increasingly aware of their rights, and know how to protect them through advocacy, campaigning and an activist from Zamzam IDPs camp posits—*We started by consoling each other with the sole purpose of strengthening relations within the community. Now, we speak up and continue to do so as care providers. We fight for social equity and for inclusion in peacebuilding processes. We are*

Fig. 5.4 IDP women establish income generating activities as a group (This photo was taken by the research assistant Dr. Mohamed Teabin, 2016)

confident we are going to win the fight. Thus, women have free agency, are capable of forming efficient grassroots organizations, have good negotiation skills, learn quickly by experience, and know how to fight for their rights as caregivers/providers. They should not be perceived simply as victims. It suffices to say that care work, which is naturally what women do, fosters peace.

Do women play an important role in peacebuilding? If yes, what are the contributions made by this role in peacebuilding? The participants thought women are indispensable to the peace process. They contribute massively to peacebuilding as caregivers through care work, though it remains unrecognized and undervalued. In IDPs camps, they form solidarity groups that campaign for peace. *We care for a peaceful society and incite solidarity amongst its inhabitants. Our message transcends politics.* Remenyi (2016) argues that women focus their efforts on building relationships and creating structures that establish and maintain peaceful communities. Furthermore, by creating grassroots groups, they have been able to voice their concerns, address issues of top priority, and satisfy their needs with ease.

5.7 The Ethics of Care Provision in War and Post-war

War is destructive to life and property, and in wartime special care arrangements are required for survival, in or outside IDPs camps. Caregivers believe care work is not just a duty, but is backed by moral, religious, and cultural values, which is why they are wholeheartedly committed to caregiving. Lachman (2012) postulates care ethics stems from the idea that care is a basic necessity for human existence. As seen in Darfur, wartime care work arrangements are way too complex. Unpaid care work and housework makes up care provision in most African nations. In the midst of the crises in Darfur, women and girls woke up every morning to provide care services to their families and communities, thus sowing seeds of hope, security, and prospects in the victims. Care ethic regards caring as relational, a responsibility and a need, in this light, human beings are responsible for how relationships emerge and evolve (Gasper et al. 2008). Caring has an associated emotional response but it does influence how women act towards others around them. *As caregivers, we have the power to transform dire circumstances and sow seeds of hope in the lives of the hopeless. We possess a spirit of compassion and commitment.* Gasper et al. (2008) citing the United Nations refers to human security as the security of people against serious threats to the fulfilment of their basic needs. Women still go through a lot of dangers and challenges in IDPs camps, but they need to defy all odds and make their voices heard.

Gendered roles in society are a norm, and both sexes are obligated to fulfil their roles in other to be socially accepted by society. Connell (2009) argues that gender is nominated, as such, "if we don't bring it into being, gender does not exist". Most of the interviewees believed that care work and housework are "women's work". Gerstel (2001) quotes participants in her study of women and care work—"I guess it's just my nature" or "It's the way I am, my nature". In IDPs camps, women confirmed what was postulated by Zembylas et al. (2014) that the moral element of care is responsiveness, wartime, and post-conflict caregiving entails continuous response to need, as once a need is met, the conditions are changed and there are always more needs arising. In post-conflict, women become breadwinners in addition to being caregivers; caring for their dependents, expanded families, and orphans, as well as managing household incomes and making household decisions for the first time in the absence of their male partners. In some contexts, these changes have led women to become activists, advocating for peace and long-term positive transformations in their societies (Arostegui 2013).

Gendered unpaid work is traditionally, strictly respected in Africa, with women having the sole responsibility of fulfilling unpaid care work. Around the world, women spend between three to six hours per day on unpaid care activities while men spend just half an hour to two hours (Ferrant et al. 2014). Feminist scholars and writers as far back as the 1980s have been alerting the rest of the world about the gendered aspects of care work (Zembylas et al. 2014). Blythe et al. (2013) espouses the feminist movement as they argue that foster care is a gendered activity with distinct male and female roles, the female roles involving the bulk of the care work. Robinson follow suit by firmly stating that "Care ethics exposes the ways in which dominant norms and discourses sustain existing power relations that lead to inequalities in the way in which societies determine how and on what bases care will be given and received" (Robinson 2008: 171).

Marriage is a union between two equal partners. Gendered care work and housework defeats this purpose. However, conflict can alter traditional norms and practices, leading to a change in the power structure of a society by dramatically shifting women as caregivers to male-dominated roles. In post-conflict, women become wage earners, breadwinners, and decision makers, while men are demoted. Men do perceive this shift as a threat to their power. Mahon and Robinson (2011) argue convincingly that caring relations must be understood as being shaped and constrained by relations of power. For this reason, Robinson's (2011) ethic of care calls for an interrogation of the economic, social, and political environment that is under study. Robinson (2011) explains that the ethic of care asks a critical question—What authority of power holds care in place? She cites Annette Baier (1996: 28) to answer that, relationships are steeped in power hierarchies that are in some cases masked as equal.

The position of women in the public or private realm is subjected to change with changing circumstances. The longer they stay in the public realm, for example, as job holders, the more they solidify their position. A "man's work" is capital-intensive and meant for production while a "woman's work" is labour-intensive and meant for providing services, especially care work and housework. This established stereotype is the basis for gendered labour and for women assuming the bulk of wartime unpaid care work. Stensöta (2011) states in order for the ethics of care to reach its full potential, the boundary between private and public has to be transgressed and care has to take its place as public ethics of care. The unequal distribution of unpaid care work between women and men represents an infringement on women's rights (UN 2013). Proponents of care ethics describe realms of caring such as good parenting, friendship, and community membership as relationships that foster human development, social cooperation, and the basic foundation of all morality and ethics (Whyte and Cuomo 2016). They therefore reject the idea that caring and caretaking are trivial or irrelevant in the public sphere (ibid.).

The heart of care work is its emotive aspects and the interpersonal relationships. The feminization of care is thus connected to the woman's principal responsibility as the family's caregiver/provider. A caregiver inspires trust and action. *One of the best things about being a caregiver is the privilege to share your goals and dreams with your family members and being able to give back to society. Care defines us as a society*—the women narrated. *We can lead others with our care and actions, earn their trust, and inspire them to build a safer, stronger and peaceful society together.* Communalism guides the African man's thought process and way of life. Rugged individualism is not African, an African man is part of a community (Lutz 2009). In the words of John Mbiti, "I am, because we are; and since we are, therefore I am" Ubuntu philosophy (ibid.).

To conclude, feminists tend to believe that unpaid care work results fundamentally from a view of the world that justifies male domination and maintains the oppression of women. However, feminism is not just a way of analysing power relations, but also a set of strategies for changing them. In conflict and post-conflict, care activities are many and complex. Thus, how can care work be valued? How can the women as caregivers be supported? And how can relationships be reconstructed on an equal and friendly footing? An ethic of care focuses on the realities on the ground of how care work is actually practised and deliberates on how these practices can be supported and enhanced (Sevenhuijsen et al. 2003). Care is fundamental to living and the fostering of good social relations. Obligations, responsibilities, and relations with care recipients are the ethical thoughts of care. A feminist care ethics—an approach that prioritizes the obligation of caring and meeting the needs of particular others for whom we take responsibility (Held 2006). In wartime and post-war, care work arrangements save lives, and being a caregiver is voluntary, it is neither enforced nor policed. It is driven by a sense of moral responsibility. Women are naturally predisposed towards a moral responsibility to care (Mindry 2010). Women are agents who are using their skills as caregivers to meet their responsibilities for the security of their families, and even for members of their wider communities (Robinson 2011). The commitment to achieve fairness must therefore consider the four principles of unpaid care work. As it appears, there is an ethical imperative for women as care providers to assure the full enjoyment of their human rights and to alleviate inequality that exists. As Razavi (2007) states, "the importance of the different forms of care should be recognized and valued, but without reinforcing care work as something that only women can or should do".

5.8 The Impact of Care Work on Armed Rebellion

The prevention of the creation of an armed rebellion as a topic popped up during the field survey in Darfur. It adds to caregiving and peacebuilding. Protracted crises (mostly political) in some African regions, including Darfur usually lead to armed rebellion. This is increasingly becoming a matter of great concern. Men and boys are more than likely to become rebels to fend off what they perceive to be injustice or oppression. In Darfur, some of the male population is conscripted and some willingly join the rebels. In the IDP camps in Darfur, rising rates of unemployment, poverty, insecurity, violations of human dignity, housing conditions have negative impacts on children as they grow-up in the IDP camps. Thus, they are driven to join the armed rebellion because they believe they are fighting for a just course against those who traumatized their people and drove them out of their homeland. The military can kill rebels but what they cannot kill is violent extremism—powerful and influential rebellious ideologies. Rather, the military incites and propels violent extremism. This is where women as caregivers come into the picture. This however depends on the specific socio-cultural contexts. Can women as caregivers contribute to the fight against violent extremism and armed rebellion? If yes, how? The idea of analysing the impacts of care work on armed rebellion has hitherto not been conceived by scholars. In Darfur, women as caregivers are the most efficient in combating armed rebellion. They prevent their vulnerable kids from joining the armed rebellion by constantly raising the awareness in them that violence is never the best solution to the current problems, and they instead divert their attention to joining solidarity groups in the community or to sport for example, football. In the IDPs' community, women emphasized inclusive dialogue to inform and educate at the family and community level as a solution to violent extremism. They reported that they work routinely at the community level to destroy any environments that may nurture an armed rebellion. The care and education they offer delicate and vulnerable adolescents is vital to determining what they become tomorrow. One of the women added—*Although my son now is a young man, I still have a duty to do what I must to prevent him from joining the armed rebels.* Teenagers are innocent and the most vulnerable to join an armed rebellion. At this stage, mothers as caregivers make sure they develop close relationships with their sons. A mother explains—*I claim full responsibility for the future of my children. I do not want my children to be dragged into the abyss.* A widow with four children continues—*As a mother, I have ability to recognize early signs of violent extremism in my sons. I would rather lock them up inside the house that let them go astray. I keep a close eye on them to ensure they stay away from those that may seek to conscript them.* Some of the participants explained how they practically handle the reality on the ground. A mother of four teenagers stated—*the conflict obligated us to change the manner in which care for and bring up our sons to prevent them from developing violent tendencies.* Another woman who succeeded in bringing back her two sons who became rebels said—*Let us forgive them and grant them the opportunity to redeem themselves. As their mother, I care to lessen the damage done to them and to build back their self-confidence towards being well behaved, to engage them in nonviolent actions so they can help build a more peaceful future.*

Women as care givers teach their children cultural values from their childhood to their adulthood. These values prevent their absorption of extremist ideas that motivates joining armed rebellion. The identification of good practices can encourage joint actions and effective collective responses. This could provide guidance to decision makers and peacebuilders on how to prevent violent rebellion. Women as primary carers for their children, adolescents, young adults, and adults increase their ability to successfully confront violent extremism. However, not all women are equal to the tasks, endangering their children. Thus, women as caregivers need to be recognized, supported, and empowered.

The concept of caregivers and armed rebellion is absent in published literature. The role women as caregivers play in countering armed rebellion in conflict and post-conflict is a missing link that needs thorough investigation. Thus, a systematic research needs to be conducted to fully grasp this interrelation.

Note

1. The 1998 Rome Statute of the International Criminal Court (ICC) defines rape and any other form of sexual violence of comparable gravity as a crime against humanity or act of genocide. http://legal.un.org/icc/statute/99_corr/2.htm.

Bibliography

Abdollahpour, I., S. Nedjat, and Y. Salimi. 2018. Positive Aspects of Caregiving and Caregiver Burden: A Study of Caregivers of Patients with Dementia. *Journal of Geriatric Psychiatry and Neurology* 31 (1): 34–38.

Al-Safi, A. 2007. *Traditional Sudanese Medicine—A Primer for Health Care Providers, Researchers and Students.* Khartoum: Dar al-Azza.

Appiah, E.K., A. Arko-Achemfuor, and O.P. Adeyeye. 2018. Appreciation of Diversity and Inclusion in Sub-Sahara Africa: The Socioeconomic Implications. *Cogent Social Sciences* 4 (1): 1–12.

Arostegui, J. 2013. Gender, Armed Conflict, and Peace-Building: How Armed Conflict Can Catalyze Positive Change for Women. *Gender & Development* 21 (3): 533–549. Published Online 11 November 2013. http://dx.doi.org/10.1080/13552074.2013.846624.

Atim, T., D. Mazurana, and A. Marshak. 2018. Women Survivors and Their Children Born of Wartime Sexual Violence in Northern Uganda. *Disasters* 42 (1): S61–S78.

Bakari, S., and F. Leach 2007. Hijacking Equal Opportunity Policies in a Nigerian College of Education: The Micro-Politics of Gender. *Women's Studies International Forum* 30: 85–96. Published Online March 2007. https://doi.org/10.1016/j.wsif.2007.01.006.

Berry, M.E. 2018. *From Violence to Mobilization: War, Women, and Political Power in Rwanda and Bosnia-Herzegovina.* Cambridge: Cambridge University Press.

Blackden, C.M., and Q. Wodon. 2006. Gender, Time Use, and Poverty in Sub-Saharan Africa. Working Paper 73, The World Bank, Washington, DC.

Blythe, S., E. Halcomb, L. Wilkes, and D. Jackson. 2013. Caring for Vulnerable Children: Challenges of Mothering in the Australian Foster Care System. *Contemporary Nurse* 44 (1): 87–98.

Bouta, T., G. Frerks, and I. Bannon. 2005. *Gender, Conflict, and Development.* Washington, DC: World Bank.

Brimblecombe, N., J. Fernandez, M. Knapp, A. Rehill, and R. Wittenberg. 2018. Review of the International Evidence on Support for Unpaid Carers. *Journal of Long-Term Care*, 25–40. Published Online 1 September 2018. https://doi.org/10.21953/lse.ffq4txr2nftf.

Buchanan-Smith, M., and S. Jaspars. 2007. Armed Conflict, Camps and Coercion: The Ongoing Livelihoods Crisis in Darfur. *Disasters* 31 (S1): 57–76.

Cerrato, J., and E. Cifre. 2018. Gender Inequality in Household Chores and Work-Family Conflict. *Frontiers in Psychology* 9: 1330. Published Online 3 August 2018. https://doi.org/10.3389/fpsyg.2018.01330.

Connell, R.W. 2009. *Gender (Polity Short Introductions)*, 2nd ed. Cambridge: Polity Press.

Daly, M., and J. Lewis. 2000. The Concept of Social Care and the Analysis of Contemporary Welfare States. *The British Journal of Sociology* 51 (2): 281–298. Published Online June 2000. https://doi.org/10.1111/j.1468-4446.2000.00281.x.

Dirar, H.A. 1993. *The Indigenous Fermented Foods of the Sudan: A Study in African Food and Nutrition.* Wallingford, UK: CAB International.

Domínguez-Serrano, M. 2012. Unpaid Care Work in Africa. Foundation BBVA, Working Papers Series, Working Paper, No. 6.

Eagly, A.H., and W. Wood. 2012. Social Role Theory. In *Handbook of Theories of Social Psychology*, ed. A.M. Paul, A. Van Lange, W. Kruglanski, and E.T. Higgins, 458–476. Los Angeles: Sage Publications Ltd.

El-Bushra, J.I., and M.G. Sahl. 2005. Cycles of Violence: Gender Relations and Armed Conflict. Printed for ACORD—Agency for Co-operation and Research in Development (ACORD) by Ramco Printing Works, Nairobi, Kenya.

Elliott, C.C., B.N. Mtobesya, and R.A. Cheke. 2014. Alternative Approaches to Red-Billed Quelea Quelea quelea Management: Mass-Capture for Food. *Ostrich: Journal of African Ornithology* 85 (1): 31–37.

Elson, D. 1999. Labor Markets as Gendered Institutions: Equality, Efficiency and Empowerment Issues. *World Development* 27 (3): 611–627.

Eyben, R. 2012. The Hegemony Cracked: The Power Guide to Getting Care onto the Development Agenda. Working Paper, 411, 1–29, Institute of Development Studies (IDS), Brighton.

Fauziana, R., R. Sambasivam, J.A. Vaingankar, E. Abdin, H.L. Ong, M. Tan, S.A. Chong, and M. Subramaniam. 2018. Positive Caregiving Characteristics as a Mediator of Caregiving Burden and Satisfaction with Life in Caregivers of Older Adults. *Journal of Geriatric Psychiatry and Neurology* 31 (6): 329–335.

Ferrant, G., L.M. Pesando, and K. Nowacka. 2014. Unpaid Care Work: The Missing Link in the Analysis of Gender Gaps in Labor Outcomes. Issue Paper, OECD Development Center.

Folbre, N., and J.A. Nelson. 2000. For Love or Money—Or Both? *Journal of Economic Perspectives* 14 (4): 123–140.

Gasper, D., and T. Truong. 2008. Development Ethics Through the Lenses of Caring, Gender, and Human Security. Working Paper, No. 459, Institute of Social Studies, Netherlands.

Gasper, D., L.J.G. van der Maesen, T. Truong, and A. Walker. 2008. Human Security and Social Quality: Contrasts and Complementarities. Working Paper, No. 462, Institute of Social Studies, Netherlands.

Gerstel, N. 2001. Men's Caregiving Gender and the Contingent Character of Care. *Gender and Society* 15(2): 197–217. Published Online April 2001. https://doi.org/10.1177/089124301015002003.

Gilligan, C. 1982. *In A Different Voice: Psychological Theory and Women's Development*. Boston and Cambridge, MA: Harvard University Press.

Held, V. 2006. *The Ethics of Care: Personal, Political, and Global*. Oxford: Oxford University Press.

Himmelweit, S., and A. Plomien. 2014. Feminist Perspectives on Care: Theory, Practice and Policy. In *The Sage Handbook of Feminist Theory*, ed. M. Evans, C. Hemmings, M. Henry, H. Johnstone, S. Madhok, A. Plomien, and S. Wearing, 446–464. London: Sage.

Hirway, I. 2015. Unpaid Work and the Economy: Linkages and Their Implications. *Indian Journal of Labour Economics* 58 (1): 1–21. Published Online December 2015. https://doi.org/10.1007/s41027-015-0010-3.

Hobbs, M.H., and C. Rice. 2018. *Gender and Women's Studies: Critical Terrain*, 2nd ed. Canada: Women's Press.

Ibnouf, F.O. 2009. The Role of Women in Providing and Improving Household Food Security in Sudan: Implications for Reducing Hunger and Malnutrition. *Journal of International Women's Studies* 10 (4): 144–167.

Ibnouf, F.O. 2012. The Value of Women's Indigenous Knowledge in Food Processing and Preservation for Achieving Household Food Security in Rural Sudan. *Journal of Food Research* 1 (1): 238–253. Published Online 1 February 2012. https://doi.org/10.5539/jfr.v1n1p238.

Ibnouf, F.O., and C.L. Manyungwa. 2019. Gender Stereotypes in Popular Linguistic Resources: Examples from Sudan and Malawi. In the process to publish in a peer-reviewed journal.

Idang, G.E. 2015. African Culture and Values. *Phronimon* 16 (2): 97–111. Online Version ISSN 1561-4018.

ILO—International Labor Organization. 2018. *Women and Men in the Informal Economy: A Statistical Picture*, 3rd ed. Geneva: ILO. https://www.ilo.org/.

Kalabamu, F. 2006. Patriarchy and Women's Land Rights in Botswana. *Land Use Policy* 23 (3): 237–246. Published Online July 2006. https://doi.org/10.1016/j.landusepol.2004.11.001.

Kinnear, K.L. 2011. *Contemporary World Issues: Women in Developing Countries: A Reference Handbook*. Santa Barbara, CA: ABC-CLIO.

Kumar, K. 2001. Civil Wars, Women and Gender Relations: An Overview. In *Women and Civil War: Impact, Organizations, and Action*, ed. K. Kumar, 5–26. London, CO: Lynne Rienner.

Kynaston, C. 1996. The Everyday Exploitation of Women Housework and the Patriarchal Mode of Production. *Women's Studies International Forum* 19 (3): 221–237.

Lachman, V.D. 2012. Applying the Ethics of Care to Your Nursing Practice. *Medsurg Nursing* 21 (2): 112–116.

Lutz, D.W. 2009. African Ubuntu Philosophy and Global Management. *Journal of Business Ethics* 84 (Supplement 3: Global and Contextual Values for Business in a Changing World): 313–328.

Mahon, R., and F. Robinson. 2011. *Feminist Ethics and Social Policy: Towards a New Global Political Economy of Care*. Vancouver: UBC Press.

Mani, R. 2011. Women, Art and Post-conflict Justice. *International Criminal Law Review* 11: 543–560.

Marphatia, A.A., and R. Moussié. 2013. A Question of Gender Justice: Exploring the Linkages Between Women's Unpaid Care Work, Education, and Gender Equality. *International Journal of Educational Development* 33: 585–594. Published Online November 2013. https://doi.org/10.1016/j.ijedudev.2013.05.005.

McCarthy, L. 2018. "There Is No Time for Rest": Gendered CSR, Sustainable Development and the Unpaid Care Work Governance Gap. *Business Ethics: A European Review* 27 (4): 337–349. Published Online 27 September 2018. https://doi.org/10.1111/beer.12190.

Merry, S.E. 2009. *Gender Violence: A Cultural Perspective*. Chichester: Wiley-Blackwell.

Mindry, D. 2010. Engendering Care: HIV, Humanitarian Assistance in Africa, and the Reproduction of Gender Stereotypes. *Culture, Health and Sexuality* 12 (5): 555–568. Published Online 4 September 2014. https://doi.org/10.1080/13691051003768140.

Mirghani, A.M. 2007. Utilization of Non-Conventional Food Resources During Disasters in Sudan. MSc Thesis, Desertification and Desert Cultivation Studies Institute (DADCSI), University of Khartoum, Khartoum.

Moussié, R., and L. Alfers. 2016. Women Informal Workers Demand Child Care: Shifting Narratives on Women's Economic Empowerment in Africa. *Agenda* 32 (1): 119–131.

Newbury, C., and H. Baldwin. 2001. Profile: Rwanda—Civil War, Women and Gender Relations: Overview. In *Women and Civil War: Impact, Organizations, and Action*, ed. K. Kumar, 27–38. London, CO: Lynne Rienner.

Parpart, J.L. 2017. Imagined Peace, Gender Relations and Post-conflict Transformation. In *Women, Gender Equality, and Post-conflict Transformation: Lessons Learned, Implication for the Future. Part One: Theory and Framework*, ed. J.P., Kaufman and K.P. Williams, 2nd ed., 51–72. London and New York: Routledge and Taylor & Francis Group.

Peacock, D. 2003. Men as Partners: Promoting Men's Involvement in Care and Support Activities for People Living with HIV/AIDS. Paper Prepared for the United Nations Expert Group Meeting on 'The Role of Men and Boys in Achieving Gender Equality', 21–24 October, Brazil.

Raghuram, P. 2016. Locating Care Ethics Beyond the Global North. *ACME: An International Journal of Critical Geographies* 15 (3): 511–533.

Rahimaghaee, F., K. Hatamopour, K. Seylani, and V. Delfan. 2016. Nurses' Perceptions of Care During Wartime: A Qualitative Study. *International Nursing Review* 63 (2): 218–225. Published Online 6 February 2016. https://doi.org/10.1111/inr.12240.

Ramaswamy, S. 2005. India's Crisis of Governance: The Women's Perspective. *Policy and Society* 24 (3): 122–141.

Rantalaiho, L., T. Heiskanen, P. Korvajärvi, and M. Vehviläinen. 1997. Studying Gendered Practices. In *Gendered Practices in Working Life*, ed. L. Rantalaiho and T. Heiskanen. London: Palgrave Macmillan.

Razavi, S. 2007. The Political and Social Economy of Care in a Development Context: Conceptual Issues, Research Questions and Policy Options. Gender and Development, Paper No. 3. UNRISD, Geneva.

Rehn, E., and E.J. Sirleaf. 2009. Focus: Women, Gender and Armed Conflicts in ADC. *Gender Policy*. https://www.oecd.org/dac/gender-development/44896284.pdf.

Remenyi, K. 2016. Does the Inclusion of Women in Peace Building Processes Make a Difference? E-International Relations. https://www.e-ir.info.

Robinson, F. 2008. The Importance of Care in the Theory and Practice of Human Security. *Journal of international Political Theory* 4 (2): 167–188.

Robinson, F. 2011. *The Ethics of Care: A Feminist Approach to Human Security.* Philadelphia: Temple University Press.

Samman, E., E. Presler-Marshall, N. Jones, T. Bhatkal, C. Melamed, M. Stavropoulou, and J. Wallace. 2016. Women's Work: Mothers, Children and the Global Childcare Crisis. Report, Overseas Development Institute (ODI), London.

Schofield, H., S. Bloch, H. Herrman, B. Murphy, J. Nankervis, and B. Singh (eds.). 1998. *Family Caregivers: Disability, Illness and Ageing (1998).* St Leonards, NSW, Australia: Allen and Unwin in Association with VicHealth, the Victorian Health Promotion Foundation.

Seguino, S. 2011. Help or Hindrance? Religion's Impact on Gender Inequality in Attitudes and Outcomes. *World Development* 39 (8): 1308–1321.

Sevenhuijsen, S., V. Bozalek, A. Gouws, and M. Minnar-McDonald. 2003. South African Social Welfare Policy: An Analysis Using the Ethic of Care. *Critical Social Policy* 23 (3): 299–321.

Shulika, L.S., and L. Shulika. 2016. Women and Peace Building: From Historical to Contemporary African Perspectives. *Ubuntu: Journal of Conflict Transformation* 5 (1): 7–31.

Stensöta, H.O. 2011. A Public Ethics of Care for Public Administration and Implementation. A Paper Presented at the Northwestern Political Science Conference, April 20–22, in San Antonio, Texas.

Stiglitz, J., A. Sen, and J.P. Fitoussi. 2007. Report on the Commission on the Measurement of Economic Performance and Social Progress, Paris: Commission on the Measurement of Economic Performance and Social Progress.

UN—United Nations. 2013. Extreme Poverty and Human Rights: Unpaid Care Work and Women's Human Rights. Sepulveda Carmona, M. The Special Rapporteur's Report to the 68th session of the General Assembly (A/68/293).

Whyte, K.O., and C. Cuomo. 2016. Ethics of Caring in Environmental Ethics: Indigenous and Feminist Philosophies. In *The Oxford Handbook of Environmental Ethics*, ed. Stephen M. Gardiner and Allen Thompson, April 2016. https://doi.org/10.1093/oxfordhb/9780199941339.013.22.

Zembylas, M., V. Bozalek, and T. Shefer. 2014. Tronto's Notion of Privileged Irresponsibility and the Re-conceptualization of Care: Implications for Critical Pedagogies of Emotion in Higher Education Gender and Education. http://dx.doi.org/10.1080/09540253.2014.901718.

CHAPTER 6

Peacebuilding Through the Care Work Lens

6.1 No One Should Be Left Behind

Peace cannot be achieved for a community without the participation of its inhabitants. Peace is more than just the termination of armed conflict. It requires that no one should be left behind and no human rights should be ignored.[1] The "leave no one behind" concept is about whether a person's characteristics (inherent or perceived) exclude them from the opportunities enjoyed by others (Stuart et al. 2016). Women are one of the groups mostly being left behind (excluded) in peacebuilding processes in Africa. Between 1990 and 2010, only 7% of agreements, in which the UN was a third party, referenced women (Powell 2017: 285). What necessary measures are already in place to increase the representation of women in peacebuilding at all levels? Feminist scholars challenged the absence, exclusion, and marginalization of women's experiences, voices, and perspectives both at the negotiation tables and in textbooks (Sharoni 2010). The perception of women as "victim of war" fails to fully recognize the "diverse experiences" of women within conflict, particularly women as caregivers.

What does it take to include women as caregivers in every stage of peacebuilding? It requires the effective implementation of differential measures to make the experiences of women in armed conflict to matter in peacebuilding processes. As countries emerge from armed conflict, peacebuilding priorities are often determined behind closed doors,

F. O. Ibnouf, *War-Time Care Work and Peacebuilding in Africa*, Gender, Development and Social Change,
https://doi.org/10.1007/978-3-030-26195-5_6

in political settlements predominantly led by national and international male elites who frequently fail to incorporate local knowledge and public expectations in the decision-making process (Bell et al. 2004). Thus, they fail to address the true needs and priorities of the war-affected populations. The only way to build sustainable peace is if the process is owned and led by those with practical experiences of the conflict. It requires the creation of an inclusive working environment; the bottom–up approach ensures the active involvement of the local population than the top–down approach.

An enabling environment that facilitates the peacebuilding activities of women is a key to identifying entry points of effective intervention. In Darfur, the participants for this study emphasized that wartime care work involves being able to make and implement decisions in real time. *It would have been great if wartime care work stood out and is recognized for its importance*—they say. Although women had limited resources, and lacked professional training and support, their arrangement and provision of care work during and after war can underpin the efforts to build the conditions for positive peace. That is, care work saves lives and in turn provides security and peace.

Care work during and after armed conflict is everything women do on a daily basis that sustains their families and communities. The peace building process is directly linked to the living conditions of individuals in conflict and post-conflict. A peaceful community requires the availability of basic human necessities; if not human insecurity will be the order of the day. Putting an end to violence is not enough, positive peace requires pragmatic community building that guarantees human security. Community building encompasses the provision of basic catering and educational facilities, thus creating conducive environments for peace. Robinson (2011) demonstrates how the responsibilities of sustaining life are central to the struggle for basic human security. The human security concept challenges the traditional view of state security, the very essence of human security means to respect human rights (Björnberg 2012) and dignity. It is necessary that analysis of human insecurity starts from the conditions of women's lives (Björnberg 2012). Women continue to play an intangible and never fading away role in caregiving thus, contributing enormously to human security. The human security concept redefines the security-development nexus by placing individuals and communities, not states, at the centre of both security and development (Busumtwi-Sam 2008: 15).

Including women as caregivers in formal peace processes exposes their realities in armed conflict, thus drawing attention to the role women play in ensuring the survival of their family and community members. It seems that, until a significant number of the peace negotiators are women, will gender inequality, especially in care work, rape, and sexual violence, and the exclusion of women from formal duties be earnestly addressed. The need to rid women of the bulk of care work, to empower them, and to achieve gender equality is recognized by the SDGs—Target 5.4. Evidence demonstrates that when women participate in peace building processes, the decisions arrived at, are more likely to be adopted. The majority of the IDPs are women (Manchanda 2004). They possess a better understanding of the surrounding circumstances, thus are better placed to effectively carry on peace works. Their involvement in peacebuilding challenges norms that identify care work as a "woman's work". It is usually assumed that fast change is impossible, however complexity theory accounts that small changes may have large effects on unstable systems (Walby 2007: 464). This is supported by the African proverb—*if you think that you are too small to make a difference, and then you have not spent a night with a mosquito*. Recognizing unpaid care work is the first step needed for change to happen (Maestre and Thorpe 2016). Change starts with knowing and ends with doing.

Peacebuilding should be inclusive with its benefits enjoyed by all. Poorly executed peace work can result to the recurrence of conflict, gender inequality, violence against women, food insecurity, migration, and even environmental degradation. Unpaid care work is physically and emotionally onerous and time-consuming. Since women carry the bulk of this work, it entails less time is available for them to formally participate in peacebuilding, unlike men, and thus they lose the opportunity to formally state their worries, especially the unfairness in unpaid care work shared responsibilities. Gender equality cannot be achieved without addressing this unfairness which has a causal relationship with gender inequality, lack of access to formal education and employment for women, violence against women, and the exclusion of women from formal peace processes. It is relatively easier for men to accept gender bias against women and the exclusion of women from formal peacebuilding processes than to redress these issues. Culture and religion also prevent women from formally participating in peace processes. Many African communities have patriarchal family structures claimed to be informed by religion, when actually these structures are retrograde customs and traditions. Some men impinge on the rights of their wives as individuals, except on those rights the men have bestowed upon their wives. Some women are ignorant and tend to accept their fate—*Men have the final say; they are always right and women are meant to always agree with them.* There are petitions for the removal of obstacles deterring women from formal peace work, and to promote their participation in the peace processes. It requires concrete actions from policymakers to remove the barriers women face in engaging in peace processes. A shift in gender roles empowers women as decision makers (Sikod 2007: 59) and gives them autonomy over the decision to participate in peace work.

Gender inequality restrains women from unlocking their full potentials. Worldwide, gender inequality deprives women of the freedom of choice in many aspects of their lives (Weiss 2003: 582). It originates in turn at the family level, then the community, and finally the whole nation. Integrating women as caregivers into the conflict resolution and reconciliation efforts involves identifying and addressing inequalities of care work sharing. This integration should be implemented from the start and not as an afterthought. Acknowledging women as caregivers in peacebuilding processes means gender equality and the respect of the rights of women would be made a priority, alongside the provision of time-saving devices that ease care work. Because of their capacity to provide care, women should be empowered in peacebuilding and post-conflict reconstruction strategies so that they can voice out their concerns and priorities.

6.2 Bottom–Up Peacebuilding Practices

This study brings to light the implementation of peacebuilding processes from the grassroots and the work women perform as caregivers. Women are excluded from formal peace processes, but they are prominent actors in the informal and grassroots peacebuilding activities (Porter 2008). In war, women endure most of the care work than men, food provision for children and the infirm, while at the same time maintaining social and political activities as the men are in the battlefields (Pankhurst 2003). Caregiving and peacebuilding are both sides of the same coin. Experience shows that peace works should be implemented using the bottom–up approach with support from the top–down approach to attain sustainable positive peace. Peace processes need to begin with the local citizens in order to give clarity to their interests and concerns (Young et al. 2009). Women as caregivers are necessary to achieving any type of sustainable peace. The astounding achievement of women in Rwanda after years of genocide is living a proof the grassroots peacebuilding by women as caregivers are the most successful. After the hideous Rwandan genocide, women immediately responded with concrete actions in order to mitigate the dire circumstances by adopting orphans, becoming family heads and formed the Unity Club (Adeogun and Muthuki 2017). This is just one of their success stories in Africa. In South Sudan, women's organizations are also successful in sustainable peacebuilding with 30% quota constitutionally established, and as a consequence economically empowering the South Sudanese women, among other things (ibid.). "Peace that is supported and consolidated at the grassroots is more likely to be sustainable than one negotiated among elites" (Karam 2000).

Women as caregivers nurture and constitute their families, and in turn their communities which are the smallest yet strongest constituents that make up the entire nation. In Africa, woman and nation are synonyms, that is why a nation is referred to as a mother (Ebila 2015 cited in Adeogun and Muthuki 2017). A family is the primary social institution, a community is made up of families and care work is the heart of the family. Women as caregivers rely on mutually beneficial social relations to fulfil care work duties for their families and community. They are guided by societal rules embodied in culture and ethical norms. A fundamental moral value for Ubuntu is identification with others, that is, enjoying a sense of togetherness and coordinating behaviour to realize common goals (Metz and Gaie 2010). Peacebuilding is about building relationships and solidarity within the society during hard times. Thus, care can create peace in lives every day.

The social relationships among IDPs are solidified by their current predicament as is evident in IDPs camps. These camps form a common ground for cooperation and basically for being each other's keeper. Women as caregivers in these camps collaborate with each other to render care—*We all experience the same agony and so we work together to break the circle of inflicting pain on each other when we are on opposing sides. Collaboration is essential for our existence and it is what we do.* These harmonious relationships build trust and a common ground for collective peace actions. In Africa, women are regarded as the family flagship for its permanency, they continuously support families and communities morally and financially (Shulika and Shulika 2016). Women as caregivers are pivotal in creating a just and equitable society through the upkeep of their families. Thus, their exclusion from formal peacebuilding processes leads to the creation of peace that is not sustainable. As advocated by Adeogun and Muthuki (2017), since the nation is not made up of a single sex, women should also be considered as significant in the construction of a peaceful society. The representation of both men and women equally in formal peacebuilding processes should be of utmost importance for the sake of reaching and achieving durable and sustainable peace. For the implementation process for peace to be real, it should start from the level of the family, considering care work, and work its way up from there.

Long-lasting peace needs to be implemented pragmatically, not by following standards determined by the country's political elites who so often do not experience the horrid realities of conflict. Simply put, you cannot build a house starting from the roof, when a house is built to last, the foundation must be solid. Cordona et al. (2012) emphasize on the adoption of the bottom–up approach to peacebuilding; starting successively from the individual, to the household, community, and finally the nation (cited in Erzurum and Eren 2014: 251). A bottom–up approach brings to light the lives of people in conflict and post-conflict as they adapt to changing circumstances by changing care work provision considering the limited resources. It entails understanding how armed conflicts change perceptions, relations, and conditions of care arrangements on the ground. Positive peace needs diverse actors to build, especially women as caregivers, who play a crucial role in forging peaceful coexistence. These women should also be involved in policy making to help incorporate wartime care work in policies.

No sustainable peace has been attained by solely employing the top–down approach. Linking wartime care work to peacebuilding opens a new knowledge domain for debates on better peacebuilding. Practical experiences, knowledge, and skills of caregivers will be given much thought. A clearer picture of the realities of the situation and the importance of care work will be painted, providing peace practitioners with physical evidence needed for intervention and decision-making.

6.3 The Most Silenced Needs to Be Heard

Conflict influences the nature of care work, that is, care needs become more specific, urgent, and extreme. In Darfur, the time spent in performing housework has increased substantially. The women interviewed did mention that they are the sole providers for their families and orphans during and after conflict. They take care of the sick, disabled, wounded, and dying. These situations require "intensive responses" as noted in the UN Women research, that a majority of these women are widows surviving on very little of everything. The women as caregivers insist—*We never ignore the needy or turning blind eyes to their need of care.*

Women are not just mere victims or vulnerable individuals in war. They are strong in providing care services to their families and community under trying circumstances to ensure their survival and protection. As Maestre and Thorpe (2016) advocates "care work is a social good that sustains society". Women as caregivers need to be honoured for their crucial contributions to their families and communities. Their recognition in formal peacebuilding as invaluable stakeholders will strengthen their rights and well-being. However, their voices remain unheard. They are indispensable actors in negotiations and peace works for sustainable peace, still they are under-represented in peacebuilding and reconstruction strategies. However, because the lessons learned from most of the painstaking informal peacebuilding work done by women on the ground have not been institutionalized and thus rarely influence national and global policies on war and peace, their knowledge, ideas, and experiences remain at best marginalized, and at worst invisible (Alaga 2010). Recognizing and acknowledging the role of women in unpaid care arrangements and provision, and the need to address the increased care needs in wartime can bring about far-reaching efforts and impacts that create sustainable peace.

There is a growing body of feminist discourse establishing that war and peace are gendered activities, and consequently women's experiences, responses, and needs are different, which are often overlooked by national and international policy-makers (Manchanda 2005). Although women and men were affected by the same armed conflict, there are marked variances between them in their experiences. Unpaid care work has been painted by the participants for this study as one of the most critical building blocks that makes or breaks a lasting peace. Care work arrangements are a daily process; peace is something that needs to be built into the everyday activities and efforts that aim to save life. It is like collecting blocks every day to build safe rooms during the dire conditions.

Robinson (2011) focusing on gender and caring in the context of human (in)security comes closest to care work during and after armed conflict. Care work directs human relations and interdependence which are necessary to achieve well-being and security, and is best for women in war and post-war situations, instead of trying to adapt women to already existing social systems designed for and by men. The link between wartime care work and peacebuilding points out that there is no positive peace without justice, thus the silenced voices of caregivers must be heard. Without a voice, women's concerns are neither prioritized nor resolved (Porter 2003: 249). They need to be equally represented; their opinions equally taken into consideration, thus need for an enabling environment where women as caregivers can be equally active in formal peace processes.

This begs the question: how can women be granted audience in formal peacebuilding processes? Peacemakers and practitioners need to ensure their effective participation, in line with the UNSCR 1325 and SDG's Target 5.4. They need to listen to caregivers in order to understand and prioritize their needs, shine a light on unpaid care and give it the credit it deserves, and identify the effects of gender inequality on women as caregivers. Giving a voice to the voiceless will expose the actual experiences of women as caregivers in war and post-war, and will lead to the achievement of a just and lasting peace. Therefore, wartime care work needs to be consistently included in the peacebuilding agenda.

There is a need to develop solutions that are fair and just and should be highly considered. Understanding the diverse roles of caregivers can easily lead to a response that is sensitive to the voiceless. Concerted lobbying and advocacy work, by civil and non-governmental organizations, can be another powerful entry point for granting the voiceless caregivers a seat in peacebuilding and post-conflict reconstructions, encouraging them to speak up and speak out, empowering them to achieve their real potential. This is necessary for a social transformation, especially in a society with deep-rooted traditions and cultural practices. Every voice must be heard for a just and lasting peace. This also requires enhancing the capacity of the local/national institutions.

6.4 Rethinking Peacebuilding Is the Only Way Forward

African regional organizations have staged an increasingly more active internal shift in matters related to peace and security, encouraged by the idea of promoting "African solutions to African problems" (Grasa and

Mateos 2010). After decades of conflict in most African countries, there is now an urgent need to include women in building peace. The continuous questioning by feminist as to why women are still absent in peace negotiations has inspired substantial efforts towards creating seats for women at the peace negotiations table (Sjoberg 2009). It is well-documented that women are still under-represented (or even absent) in the formal peace processes in most African countries (see for example, Adeogun and Muthuki 2017; Porter 2008). Women have not been fully engaged in the peacebuilding processes due to cultural stereotypes and hegemonic masculinity.

Numerous definitions of peacebuilding have been proposed since the 1990s. In international relations scholarship, it is defined as actions carried out before, during, and after violent conflict to address the root causes of the conflict which includes transforming relationships and structures (Neufeldt 2017). Peace is a much broader and deeper concept. Peace is more than the cessation of military hostilities, which is more than political stability; peace is the presence of justice and peace building entails addressing factors and forces that stand as impediments to the realization of all human rights (Young 2005). Santa-Barbara (2007: 185) defines peace as the state in which humans can maximize use of their physical, mental, and cultural resources, and which gives the most chance for happiness for most people. Women as caregivers, who have been the backbone for their family, orphans, and community during wartime, undoubtedly will lead in peacebuilding and post-conflict reconstructions. Pankhurst (2003) postulates that women have been the survivors and carers of survivors, so this seems to have given them a sustained intensity of wanting to resolve the peace question. The care work rendered to their families in wartime in a way that ensures survival and protection demonstrates their skills and capacities to cope in such situations and to build the conditions for inclusive and just peace.

Wartime care work is ignored in peacebuilding. This is due to the missing link between caregiving and peacebuilding. The vital role women as caregivers play during and after war is an indicator that the participation of women in formal peacebuilding processes at all levels will have significant positive consequences for lasting peace and reconstructions. Their emotional and social support can form the basis for peacebuilding. These women know what the local population actually needs and value peace the most, thus could employ definite methods for positive peacebuilding. Women master the wants of the community because of their daily caregiving activities; thus, they can assess the viability of peace agreements with regard to these everyday concerns (Porter 2003: 250).

Of monumental importance, involving diverse wartime experiences in peacebuilding will lead to sustainable peace over the long term as women (and girls) will see their collective interests reflected in peacebuilding initiatives—"local ownership". Noteworthy, care determines the self-development of a human being right up to their full potential; this should be linked to peacebuilding. Caregivers work out of sheer sympathy and empathy as seen in Darfur. The real challenge here is integrating their experiences into formal peacebuilding processes. In contemporary care theory, care emerges as both a complex and evolving social phenomenon, and as an enduring and inspirational moral value (Rummery and Fine 2012). This has an impact on the value and visibility of the role of women as caregivers/providers both during and in the wake of conflict, and their opportunities to participate effectively in peacebuilding and post-conflict remonstrations. Moreover, it has impacted the quality and effectiveness of post-conflict interventions, including basic services and humanitarian assistance.

The greatest numbers of war victims are women, but this is not the case when it comes to the greatest number in peace negotiations round tables, or even a significant number. Armed conflicts around the world have received considerable international attention, but a blind eye has always been given to women as peacebuilders. The men leading peace processes at all levels still exclude women, thus producing agreements that are disconnected from the realities on the ground and less likely to be successful and popularly supported. This is typical of the African continent where men largely dominate in numbers as peacekeepers, peace negotiators, politicians, peacebuilders, and even as post-armed conflict constructionists. Women are on the losing end. However, it is not about women winning in dominance, but about being given an equal opportunity to participate in formal peacebuilding processes. The issue of having "power over" the men is exactly what feminism is trying to get rid of; it is about giving equal "power to" the women or sharing equal "power with" the men. In this light, the society after war can be rebuilt for all, and the unequal structures can be addressed outright. As evident in Darfur, power shifts overtime, for example, women become breadwinners and decision makers for the household in post-conflict. In the absence of men in armed conflict, women assume their responsibilities as the head of the family (Manchanda 2005).

Peace work is often criticized for being implemented based on theory rather than on practical experience. Care work is the practical experience, and thus caregivers should work hand in glove with and as formal peacebuilders for the attainment of sustainable peace. For peacebuilding to be sustainable, it should reflect the realities on the ground. In Darfur, women invest most of their time on care work, performed based on the needs on the ground. Manchanda (2005) adds that women in conflict areas carry the bulk of work for the survival of their families with little or no food, shelter, basic services, education, and means of livelihood. The drawback associated in integrating care work into the peacebuilding agenda is the impression that care is purely a private matter. Eliminating this ideology will bring care work and women as caregivers in wartime into the limelight. Care is the invisible base of the system, which is only, noticed when it is lacking (Orozco 2009). Peace is often recognized by its absence (Barash and Webel 2009). If this is the case, then care is an integral part of peace. Care is more primarily connected to the daily practices to achieve well-being. Peace is the presence of well-being (Barash and Webel 2009). This is often neglected by peacebuilders and practitioners. Peacebuilding involves a process comprised of various functions and roles, it often entails a wide range of sequential activities, including among others, the advancement of human rights (Jeong 2005).

Unfair wartime care work burden on women, the violation of their rights as individuals and gender inequality will never be sufficiently addressed unless women are equally present in number at peace negotiations tables and are fully engaged in peace works and reconstructions. Krause et al. (2018) posit that apart from respecting the rights of women by equally involving them in peace processes, scholars emphasize the usefulness of the social knowledge and experiences of women during war in peacebuilding, among others. At least women's presence in the peace process will guarantee that wartime care work issues will be on the agenda. Gender inequality needs to be taken into account when making social policies, or it might end up reappearing or exacerbated. Social policy can shape the care that will be provided, and in doing so, influences peacebuilding. Achieving a more egalitarian balance of unpaid care work is likely to require changes on several fronts, from a greater recognition of women's disproportionate share of this work to the importance of women's well-being and access to other rights (Marphatia and Moussié 2013).

The absence of violence alone cannot create sustainable peace. Negative peace describes the absence of active armed conflict, while positive peace is a much broader concept that encompasses economic and social well-being as well as cultural identity (Guttieri and Piombo 2007). Barash and Webel (2009) define positive peace as "a social condition in which exploitation is minimized or eliminated and in which there is neither overt violence nor the more subtle phenomenon of underlying structural violence". On the other hand, Erzurum and Eren (2014: 238) cites that positive peace requires the absence of indirect and structural violence such as gender inequality. Building peace needs to be through personal struggles not by being spoon fed, as women revealed during group discussions. Positive peace implies a situation in which the local people have a sense of empowerment, participation, and accountability (Guttieri and Piombo 2007). Positive Peace is the attitudes, institutions, and structures that are associated with creating and sustaining peaceful and resilient societies. The feminists have redefined peace by including the crucial dimension of gender relations in its realm (Pitanguy 2011). Gender equality is the base for peace processes. Women as caregivers'/providers' contribution to the peacebuilding processes need to go beyond defining peace as the absence of violent conflict and focus on positive peace and the four principles of care. Positive peace implies serious changes at many different levels of society in order for peace to be sustainable. Positive peace is understood as social justice at all levels of society (Confortini 2010). Peace needs to become more responsive to the requirements of local contexts and actors and recognize the needs of everyone.

There is a pressing need to include unpaid care work into the peacebuilding processes both theoretically and practically. The value of care work has not been reflected in peace negotiations or peacebuilding. Care work is the basis of survival of war-affected populations, and is linked to family and community well-being, thus it provides new insights into conflict transformation. Women as caregivers have a strong impact on the IDP community's solidarity, resilience, and local security. They are poised to generate compelling peace, and continue to take matters into their own hands for empowerment and progress. In Darfur, women organized groups to live in relative peace and stability in IDPs camps. The interviewed women revealed, "*We rise above tribal differences and think as a unit and work to build a peaceful environment for the future of our children*". It is vital that diverse experiences and especially the experiences of women as caregivers be represented in peacebuilding.

Lastly and most importantly, care work can address some of the shortcomings of peacebuilding. Because of the contentious nature of care activities, peacebuilders tend to judge who is "deserving" to be integrated in the peacebuilding process, which activities can be considered as "work", and what appoints persons to social and economic roles in post-conflict. To conclude, the fifth UN Secretary General *Pérez de Cuéllar* states: "Where women's views and experiences are absent, the political process remains incomplete". Similarly, the peace process remains incomplete if wartime care work is not considered.

6.5 In Order to Avoid Repeating the Same Mistake

Attaining sustainable peace in African regions affected by conflict is elusive. The complexity of the conflict in most African countries calls for all stakeholders to re-examine the factors that have undermined the peace efforts and correct mistakes of the previous peace agreements. In Africa, the use of military force to resolve armed conflicts surpasses the use of nonviolent peacebuilding approaches. Consequently, the results are always unsuccessful and recurrent. Such peace agreements focus mainly on how the fighting can be stopped, how former combatants are reintegrated into society, and how displaced people can return to their homes. Therefore, there is a need' to rethink the concept of peace, including methods and practices to implement positive peace so as to avoid a vicious circle. The underlying causes of conflict need to be effectively addressed to stop its recurrence. This involves addressing the needs and priorities of the population with their full participation and without gender bias, and to give all concerned stakeholders equal attention in peacebuilding and post-conflict reconstructions. Peace agreements in which women's concerns and priorities have not been well addressed may be unjust and ineffective, and may lack long-term viability (Bates 2000 cited in Tadesse et al. 2010). Women as caregivers need to be represented in conflict transformations that concern them so as to make use of their practical experiences needed for sustainable peacebuilding. This may yield positive and efficient results as well as boosts the caregivers' morale and ownership.

The number of "peace agreements" that have been signed in Darfur so far, have had very limited effect on achieving peace "on the ground". Netabay (2009) argues that, in the case of Darfur, the peace process has failed due to a number of factors; among them is the exclusiveness of participation in formal peacebuilding. The number of women in Darfur participating in peacebuilding processes so far is not proportionate to the 75% of the IDPs' population which they represent. It is time to rethink making peace work more inclusive. All conflicts are highly contextual and merit a thorough analysis which can produce a strategy that makes the most of existing stakeholders and their lived experiences. That is, including the experiences and perspectives of those who have traditionally been neglected from the peacebuilding processes. The lived experiences of women as caregivers during wartime are sorely overlooked in many peacebuilding efforts. Such practical experiences come with practical knowledge needed for pragmatic peacebuilding. Where peacebuilding disregards unpaid wartime care work, it can be detrimental for both peace outcomes and post-conflict reconstruction.

The active engagement of women in peacebuilding is essential for success. They suffer from gender-based war crimes and other offences that undermine peacebuilding. Sexual violence against women and the initiation of advocacy programs at all levels need to be made a priority by policymakers. Nonetheless, women are equally powerful agents of peace. Although women generally are seen as victims in conflict situations, they are often mothers, breadwinners, combatants, or peace activists as well (Bouta et al. 2005).

Time and again, the language that is used to describe women living in a war zone is "vulnerable" and "helpless", despite the remarkable capabilities these same women have to adapt to and survive the violence, loss, and deprivation that goes hand in hand with war (Haeri and Puechguirbal 2010). These hurdles women face justify how they are viewed—mainly as victims of war. Rather than being one of the topics to be discussed at the negotiation table between the peace practitioners, women should be guaranteed adequate inclusion in the negotiations as active participants. In this light, women should be recognized as agents and negotiators with their own voice and the importance of wartime care work should also be recognized.

Women have played a pivotal role in post-conflict social movements and civil society peacebuilding processes across diverse contexts. Women adopted a bottom–up approach within which they were largely involved in peacebuilding at grassroots level (Adeogun and Muthuki 2018). Peacebuilding efforts that are exerted by governmental and non-governmental agencies in post-conflict areas focus on a stunted peace which does not cover fighting as well as inequalities between men and women (Erzurum and Eren 2014: 238). Post-conflict social policies and gender-sensitive initiatives that facilitate an enabling working environment for women as caregivers in formal employment is critical in promoting their socio-economic status and thus achieve gender equality. Arrangements of care work during and after war, if not valued will continue to be considered as normal women's activities. There is a need to insert wartime care work in all aspects of the reconstruction and peacebuilding processes.

Women faced the realities on the ground in armed conflict and so it makes sense that they have elaborated conceptions about wartime caregiving and peace processes. Care work links to peacebuilding because it preserves lives, especially in harsh conditions. The current situation demands a new approach that goes beyond the existing conflict transformation process to seeking knowledge that can be useful for peacebuilding. Bottom–up and top–down processes need to be harmonized for peace processes to be sustainable and successful because they complement each other.

6.6 Substantial Representation of Women as Caregivers in Peace Processes

This book provides quality evidence that can support policy making and advocacy on behalf of women as caregivers which can be utilized in peacebuilding processes. It also contributes to the global knowledge on women as caregivers/providers in wartime and in the aftermath of war and to uplifting the integrity of women in peacebuilding processes. Taking a bottom–up approach, this knowledge can be used to inform peacebuilding starting from the home, to the institutions and finally the decision makers. No planning and implementation work can be effective without a thorough understanding of the reality on the ground.

Why is the representation of women as caregivers in peace making important? By and large, women experience war differently from men and bring different perspectives to peace and security issues, these differences are largely socially constructed (Powell 2017: 286). Thus, the position of women in all stages of peace processes ought to be irreplaceable. For bringing different experiences and perspectives to the peace table due to gendered social roles and the fact that (civilian) women often experience war differently from (combatant) men, women's participation in peace making will help legitimize peace processes (Powell 2017: 322). Through a focus on representation, it is possible to explore the processes of staking claims around unpaid care and domestic work to identify those whose voices are included/excluded within such processes, and how effectively they channel their claims within the policy space (Cornwall 2003 cited in Rao 2018: 738). At the expense of generalization, increasing the numbers of women (in quality and not quantity) in peace processes from the very outset can lead to better outcomes. Women cannot be simply added to the proceedings to meet quotas for the increased inclusion of women, but should instead be effectively utilized (Remenyi 2016).

Women as caregivers need to be included into peace processes to adequately represent their Interests. Krause et al. (2018) argue that the direct participation of women in peace negotiations increases the quality and durability of peace. Statistical research involving a substantial dataset shows that women's participation increases the probability that the peace agreement will last longer (O'Reilly et al. 2015). The inclusion of women at all levels of peacebuilding is an imperative; this is because the vision of sustainable peace is significantly reliant on the active involvement of the female half of the society (Shulika and Shulika 2016). Who is better placed to solve or handle the women's problem of overburden of unpaid care work during and after armed conflict than the women themselves? Which kind of women is needed at the negotiation tables? There is a need for women who have not been brainwashed by cultural practices that subordinates them to men. Most of the brainwashed women insist that what is being said by men reflects what they would have said. If women are sensitized that there are millions of them out there in need of change regarding their situation in unpaid care work and other aspects of life, then movements towards change will definitely be initiated. Gender equality is an indicator for one of the eight pillars of positive peace: the acceptance of the rights of others. Peace building entails addressing factors and forces that stand as impediments to the realization of all human rights (Young 2005: 99). Furthermore, while women are more aware of the role they can play as peacebuilders, they need to be continuously provided with capacity building on peace building tools which should be framed within their local context using mechanisms they are already familiar with.

Because women have different experiences in conflict to those of men, they also have different perspectives on how peace should be built.

This difference results from care work. Women as caregivers in wartime and its aftermath are motivated to develop new solutions to address conflict issues, shaped by their family and community needs and priorities. They are vigilant about the realities during armed conflict and take the responsibility to save lives that otherwise would be hurtled in the armed conflict. Men and women ultimately have different definitions of peace; their methodology in pursuing peaceful goals will also be different (Remenyi 2016). Peace means different things to women and men; this is important to examine when considering how the inclusion of women impacts peace building processes and outcomes. Moosa et al. (2013) found that men prioritized negative peace, focusing on "the absence of formal conflict and insecurity at all levels, as well as with the stability of formal structures, such as governing institutions and infrastructure" (cited in Remenyi 2016). Contrastingly women were more interested in peace on a local level and within the private sphere, with emphasis on family and community needs, for example "peace within the household", thus valuing positive peace over negative peace (Moosa et al. 2013 cited in Remenyi 2016). Care work is almost never recognized in peacebuilding negotiations, policies, and programs. Acknowledging care work as women are included in peacebuilding processes is a win-win situation. Thus, any interventions must be designed to reflect the interrelated nature of caregiving and peacebuilding. Unpaid care work is often referred to in post-conflict development programs but has not been given sufficient attention. Lack of implementation sustained by a lack of political will, combined with cultural conservatism, have all come together to prevent the establishment of an enabling environment for equitable peacebuilding involvement.

International peacebuilding is experiencing a pragmatic turn (De Coning 2018). Adaptive peacebuilding is an approach in which peacebuilders, together with the communities and people affected by the conflict, actively engage in a structured effort to sustain peace by employing an iterative process of learning and adaptation (De Coning 2018). It is well placed to facilitate the shift in peacebuilding towards a long-term investment in preventing conflict and sustaining peace, with a focus on strengthening the resilience of social institutions, and investing in social cohesion and related capacities that assist societies to self-sustain their peace processes (De Coning 2018). The Darfur case shows that solidarity and shared experiences of both war and displacement eased the process of living together, and belongings were shared with relatives and neighbours. There is a high level of social cohesion reflected by the widespread of inter-ethnic marriages, as indicated during the interviews and group discussions in Darfur. An inter-ethnic marriage helps in bringing about more peaceful relations between contending ethnic groups and therefore building peaceful communities. The findings are largely consistent with the social cohesion theory that, intermarriage reduces the probability of violent conflict among social groups (Smits 2010). As stated by Tadesse et al. (2010) marriage is one way of bonding two rival groups in the process of peacebuilding and conflict resolution, when two clans are connecting through marriage; it is the married woman who forms the backbone of the newly established community.

This is partly because of the low value placed on women's time. More positive outcomes can be achieved when care work concerns are mainstreamed into prevailing peacebuilding processes. Considering gender in peacebuilding also increases the chances of successful planning, implementation, and institutionalization of a post-armed conflict order (Hudson 2009: 288). The significance of care as a fundamental feature of human life and social institutions must be given full recognition (Gasper et al. 2008) in peacebuilding processes. Unpaid care work is fundamental to sustaining daily life. Building peace implies placing the processes of sustaining daily life in the centre of the peacebuilding process, that is, women as caregivers for their families and communities, their experiences, priorities, and perspectives on armed conflict. Through unpaid care work, women have succeeded to build and maintain peace at household and IDP community levels and they can bring this experience to the negotiation table. Gasper and Truong (2008) advocates that women are characteristically family "shock absorbers": they care for the ill and infirm, they enter all forms of flexible or informal work when family pressures demand it, they are pressurized in times of change to embrace purported traditions, they give to others security and comfort. Interviewed women mentioned choosing paid work close to home or more flexible, part-time jobs to allow them to mind their children, cook meals, and care for elderly relatives, without incurring additional time and financial cost. Unequal distribution of responsibilities for unpaid work between women and men within the household also translates into unequal opportunities in terms of time to participate equally in paid activities (Ferrant et al. 2014).

Feminist scholars have long focused on the experience of women as caregivers and gendered unpaid care work which contributes to the perpetuation of gender inequality. Gender-biased traditions associate girls to unpaid care work which prevents them from schooling. *The educational path is a rocky road for many girls*—this quote implies that girls may drop out of school in part because they share the care work responsibilities with their mothers or substituting for their personal care activities. Girls are expected to endure care work because it is part of their womanhood duties and a social norm. They are forced to support their mothers in unpaid care tasks unlike boys, thus an infringement on their rights to education. In this way, the existing inequality in life choices between women and men persists across generations (Marphatia and Moussié 2013). This disparity becomes a concern for "gender justice" not only because the tasks and the women who perform them are undervalued, but also because of how a disproportionately higher level of care work restricts personal growth and professional development (ibid.). Girls, like their mothers, forgo the capabilities (skills, knowledge) and autonomy (facilitated through greater confidence and voice) which may enable them to better negotiate a fairer balance between care work and other opportunities (Marphatia and Moussié 2013).

6.7 Considering an Ethic of Care—Wartime Care Work and Peacebuilding

> Security can no longer be understood in purely military terms… Rather, it must encompass economic development, social justice, environmental protection, democratization, disarmament, and respect for human rights and the rule of law —Kofi Annan (the seventh Secretary-General of the United Nations) Towards a Culture of Peace, 2001

Unpaid care work is an ethical concept that guides the behaviours of women towards their family and community during and after war. Robinson (2011) suggests that security can be critically examined by using care as a guiding moral principle. She argues that rethinking human security following the feminist Ethics of care guiding principles represents a shift of care Ethics into the arena of the international security. A critical inquiry is needed to be made into the concept of security as being more than just a problem for the state, but also as one of care and psychosocial requirements (Gasper et al. 2008). Human security shifts the traditional concept of security from the absence of war to the security of the individual; it recognizes that the basic rights of people are fundamental to the stability of the state (Parmar et al. 2014).

Valuing the role women fulfil in care work during and after war will create conducive environment for their participation in peace work. Care work is so embedded in the everyday workings of peaceful life. This point can be viewed from the perspective of Ethics of care. Feminists have long sought to challenge the invisibility of women's unpaid work; feminist Ethics provides a particularly effective means to make the invisible visible. That feminist Ethics of care could be used as a standard through which to address the devaluation of caring arrangement during wartime and its aftermath. During wartime, women are the sole care providers and care work is their responsibility of moral values. Moral reality is embedded in relations and practices of responsibility and recognition (Robinson 2011: 5) for moral relations of care for the security of particular others, those who are vulnerable and dependent (p. 8). Within the feminist scholarship, attention has been given to the link between peace and femininity. Carroll (1987) advocates for women that they play an important role as peace activists while resisting gender subordination from men that consider these women to be "natural peacemakers" because peace is "typically feminine". Therefore, the critical role that women play through their care work services should be rendered visible, and it can be argued that this qualifies them as leading voices in peace building.

Feminist Ethics of care considers relationships and interactions as the foundation of care. From a feminist ethic of care's view point, the relationships are closely connected to how questions of responsibility within the realm of these relational experiences can be understood and how the relations raise important ethical questions about care. An ethic of care perceives relationships to be of primary importance for it is through relationships that we are connected to others, we have a responsibility for sustaining these relationships, and this includes being attentive to addressing the needs of others (Linsley 2017). Thus, human relations and practices of care responsibility are inextricably linked during and after armed conflict. Relations require interdependence between those involved in caring, and it includes interactions between the care provider and the care receiver. Care ethicists claim that relationships matter morally; it is these relationships that give rise to responsibilities and practices of care (Robinson 2011). They argue that the notion of care is best understood from a perspective that focuses on the associations between people and on the contextual experiences within these relationships (Kuhse et al. 1998 cited in Green 2012). Ethical responsibilities to care in practice contribute to the survival and well-being of the family and community. In other words, it is a sense of moral responsibility that keeps women arranging care work in horrific conditions such as wartime. Ethics of feminism is based on responsibility, everyone has a sense of responsibility when faced with the needs and suffering of others, "responsible" means responding to others' needs when able (Rahele 2016). Armed conflict may leave women with little choices but continuous care work responsibilities because there is no or very limited care services available. In post-armed conflict, in addition to carrying on with their caregiving roles, they take on breadwinner roles.

Feminist Ethics gives us a clear view of the bulk of care work borne by women not adequately addressed by peacebuilders/practitioners. Since care is not recognized as an important factor in the production process, it is left to households to arrange it, as a result, the burdens of caring in individual households are typically unpaid, unrecognized, and carried out with little support (Zachorowska-Mazirkiewicz 2015). This consolidates women's position in the society as undervalued caregivers, without acknowledging their value to well-being and social security. For women, the role assigned to them by society as carers can undermine their rights and limit their opportunities, capabilities, and choices, posing a fundamental obstacle to gender equality and well-being (Esplen 2009). The Ethics of care is not restricted only to the private sphere; it also has an impact in the public arena. An African feminist ethic can be developed and the fight for public recognition must begin in the home, taking cognizance of the fact that African women face several challenges as custodians of value (Mangena 2009). Unpaid work acts as a barrier to gender equality, thus it needs to be considered in peace talks. The political and economic developments policies are concerned only with the paid economy in the public domain (men's realm) and do not adequately address unpaid care work in the private domain. In fact, this inequality is at the bases of power relations between men and women, and all other pervasive gender inequalities (Hirway 2015). Gendered care does not end when conflict comes to an end. Unequal distribution of unpaid care work violates women's right to social security as unpaid workers and the right to participation (Hirway 2015).

Care is embedded in a set of implicit cultural practices of recognizing the needs of others, and feeling responsible for addressing these needs

(Schmidt 2018). Passivity and silently accepting injustice may be seen as signs of femininity. Caregiving/providing within the feminist school of thought is linked with how women's rights and justice for women are met. Consequently, it is necessary to address these issues of injustice which render caregivers/providers invisible in peacebuilding processes. Recognition, valuing, and support for care work imply developing policies to transcend the conventional boundary of the public and the private at all levels, policies that connect the dots between private and public domains. Feminist geographer Dyck (2005) discusses how important care is in the formation of the global political economy; women's social and political status and unpaid work needs to be discussed with the same intensity as economic growth, as it is the backbone of the economic system. Hence, care provision, in addition to individuals, must be a State's responsibility to develop effective social policies guided by using feminist views to ensure nothing has been left out and women's caregiving has been given priority. Effective post-conflict strategic plans need to take into account the lessening of caregivers' burden and provide caregivers with care needed supports and resources. Social policies so far ignore the concerns of caregivers and thus have yielded very small "returns". A feminist researcher, Barbara Pini (2002: 340) contends that one of the most important challenges for feminist scholars is a need for their work to be political "to change women's lives, both at a personal level and a societal level" (cited in Liamputtong 2011: 19). Therefore, feminist researchers must undertake research for the beneficial of women, "*research for women*" instead of "*research on women*" (ibid.).

Women as caregivers are excluded from peacebuilding debates implying their needs are overlooked thus increasing their vulnerability in post-conflict. The feminist Ethics of care theoretical approach offers a point of reference from which it may be possible to rethink how wartime unpaid care work arrangement could be linked to peacebuilding processes, and therefore work towards practical action and social transformation. Within the feminist scholarship, some shed light on the marginalization of women's voices in existing debates about the nature of peace (Brock-Utne 1990). Representation can assure that the voices of women are heard. Women would make a difference and change the international agenda in peace negotiations and peacebuilding processes if they were equally represented like their male counterparts. As Razavi (2007) states "recognizing and valuing the importance of different forms of care, but without reinforcing care work as something that only women can or should do". Without caregivers' involvement, efforts to bring peace would not only lack a critical feminist's view, but would simply be inadequate and ultimately ineffective, which have been witnessed in many African cases as in Darfur.

Gasper and Truong (2008) in citing feminist care Ethics presented a multifold vision of care: first, as a moral orientation, disposition, and emotion; second, as a set of skills and understandings; third, as a social practice found in a variety of significant relations such as mothering, friendship, nursing, and citizenship; and lastly, as a socio-economic system jointly managed by private and public actors. The use of a feminist Ethics of care is essential to enlightening aspects of wartime caregiving that are often out of focus, and not given due consideration in peacebuilding and reconstruction processes. As a result of the reality of armed conflict, the social fabric of a society breaks down and a momentary power vacuum arises, which creates a battle ground for women to fill many top-ranking positions, thus, the positive effects of armed conflicts on the status of women. Women enjoy some semblance of power in the household and community. Men often leave their homes and in practice women start to take on "men's roles" in their absence. In abnormal circumstances, normal rules no longer apply. Although gender norms are difficult to change (Seguino 2011: 1317), however there are great commonalities in the transformation of gender relations in post-conflict. As Meredeth Turshen points out: 'along with its negative impacts, war also destroys the patriarchal structures of society that confine and degrade women, and opens up new doors and creates new beginnings for these women' (cited in Sidonia 2018: 189). However, most of these changes are temporary, or at least till the conflict is resolved. As stated by Arostegui (2013), the roles of women alter and expand during conflict as they participate in the struggles and take on more economic responsibilities and duties as heads of households. Despite this shift of events, when conditions return to normal, the roles of women shift from active and purposeful back to invisible and marginalized. A feminist Ethics of care is concerned with domination and subordination. Women are viewed as symbols for the family and are meant to procreate, while men are pushed into "hyper-masculine roles" in society such as peacebuilders. This hampers the efforts of women's empowerment and gender equality in post-conflict. It is unlikely to expect women to retain their rights in a sustainable manner without possessing the basic awareness, skills, and knowledge even if the rights are handed to them. In order to perform care practices, the caregiver needs sufficient education, time, and support (Engle et al. 1999). The provision of these resources by the state or society can be considered care for the caregiver (ibid.).

Understanding the values involved in care, and how its standards reject domination, are possible with the Ethics of care. The usefulness of feminist Ethics of care in thinking about peacebuilding can be accurately interpreted in the light of the context in which it is articulated. The transition from conflict to peace offers a unique opportunity for transforming institutions, structures, and relationships that hinder gender equality and justice. Everything that promotes and favours women is moral; ethical care and care theory is the basics of education in general and care Ethics should be supported to make it strategic (Rahele 2016). For any reconstruction strategy to be sustainable, it should publicize the Resolution 1325, and should make a genuine effort to establish gender equality in the community through gender mainstreaming, namely creating the space for women as caregivers to voice their concerns on how to address their needs and interests. Ensuring policies align with international commitments to gender equality. Such policies must be strengthened by a commitment to action if they are to be effective.

Feminizing care is often quoted to indicate that women are still expected to perfectly perform the role of caregivers/providers. Robinson (2011: 115) does not view an ethic of care "as a set of principles waiting to be 'applied'", as is the case with some of the frameworks in the field of Development Studies. Mahon and Robinson's (2011) argument that an Ethics of care is political and critical must be grounded into the concrete activities of real people in webs of social relations. This could have implications for the whole of post-conflict reconstruction strategies in Africa, which requires actions for well-being and social justice. Caregivers' ability to cope with difficulties and deal with care burden depends on the effective social policies, which include availability, accessibility, and affordability of quality social services.

By investigating caregiving arrangement during wartime and in the aftermath of war, using a feminist Ethics of care theoretical approach, this book inspires rethinking peacebuilding processes differently. Transformation towards a more realistic and positive representation of women in peacebuilding will lead to the acknowledgement of their contributions to unpaid work. Thus, political actions that can put caregivers' rights, empowerment, and equality among the key priorities in the peacebuilding agenda may be taken. This will lead to the recognition of the value of unpaid care work performed by women by guaranteeing them a leading voice in peace building and by recognizing care at the heart of peace, and also by the redistribution of care responsibilities equally among all social actors. By using a feminist Ethics of care theoretical approach that includes the voices of women and their conceptions of peacebuilding, this book will motivate governments to improve their planning and policies related to investment in infrastructure, to improve the provision of high-quality public services in post-conflict situations, to acknowledge unpaid care work to find more effective ways to balance it so that it can benefit women, men, families, communities, and to achieve lasting peace.

"Peace is the presence of justice" (Bendaña 2003: 8). Justice is inextricably linked with care work. Care and Justice are both values and parts of the same continuum, care serves justice and justice is a part of care. It presents a means legitimizing one of them in terms of the other. If "justice" views "care" as "to provide protection", then care consists primarily of ensuring that justice continues to reign in a society. At wartime, care is both a necessary and a sufficient condition for justice. Lloyd (2006) argues that care must be connected to justice, or we would end up in a situation where the rich care for the rich and the poor care for the poor, and care would be a random practice. Kittay (2002: 273) calls for a "caring" based on "justice" where dependency is positively acknowledged and met by a collective responsibility (cited in Kingston 2007: 28). Carol Gilligan had developed the Ethics of care in response to the Ethics of justice. Care is a moral orientation for social justice. Peace is built on justice; care forms the basis for justice. The global justice requires a conception of caring, a "caring solidarity", to complement a systemic vision (Gasper and Truong 2008).

Justice and care are two sides of a coin, the two orientations may be analytically distinguishable, but they are united in practice (Nelson 2011). Thus, justice and care seem to be complementary rather than contradictory. UNSCR 1325 and the national legislations and strategies that promote human rights and equality are extremely important but it seems that there is still a huge gap between theory and practice. As such the SDG target 5.4 may provide one useful avenue for advocacy, but it must be grounded in the lived realities of African women both as workers and carers to be relevant and effective in changing policies (Moussié and Alfers 2016). Justice cannot be served if the need for care and for economic production is not balanced in such a way that some citizens (overwhelmingly women) are disproportionately responsible for care (McKenzie 2016). In this regard, it is imperative that the needs and concerns of women be included at the outset of peace negotiations and agreements, in institutional reforms, and in the reforms of justice and security systems.

6.8 Does Conflict Open Doors of Opportunity for Gender Equality Through Care Work?

While conflicts in Africa drastically affect social and cultural structures, they can also provide a window of opportunity for addressing structural inequalities. At the crux of the matter, conflict opens up potentially transformative spaces for gender relations, and peacebuilding processes can foster rather than hinder the development of gender equality in post-conflict spaces. The challenge is to seize this opportunity to promote gender equality. It represents a light looming in the horizon for greater change for women.

Men and women have different social roles and responsibilities created by gendered labour in the public and private spheres. The division of caring responsibilities by gender has consequences for official policies, where women are natural carers (in the private and personal sphere) and men as natural providers of care (which takes place in the public sphere) (Kingston 2007: 17). Piergallini (2014) postulates that women have been attributed a "natural" capacity and desire to care, a misconception that has proved to reinforce gender inequalities by disproportionately burdening women with unpaid or low paid care work. McCarthy (2018) found out that women's unpaid care roles are located firmly in the private realm, therefore, missing a unique opportunity to contribute to gender equality. The women interviewed for this study revealed—*Loves drives me to care for my family. I do not consider caring as a job because I cannot see myself doing anything else. It is what I was meant to do.* While individuals do perform care work out of love and self-fulfilment (Folbre and Nelson 2000), the over-representation of women in this work has a detrimental effect on gender equality in myriad ways (McCarthy 2018: 340). The role change in post-conflict considerably increases the burden on women, but it may also strengthen their capacities and organizational capabilities, inducing taking on more public roles during or after conflict (Bouta et al. 2005).

The unequal distribution of care responsibilities is not an issue of the private sphere, but must be seen as also impacting the public sphere because it eliminates women from participating in formal peace processes. Gender justice requires that nobody should be expected to work harder without a corresponding compensation, simply because of their gender (Gheaus 2012). The disparity becomes a concern for "gender justice" because the disproportionately higher level of care work restricts the personal growth and professional development of women (Marphatia and Moussié 2013). Armed conflict affects traditional gender roles and relations. Thus, post-conflict development could accelerate the empowerment of women and preserve the progress made towards gender equality (Brück and Vothknecht 2011: 86). The post-armed conflict period provides the opportunity for wide-ranging public sector reforms: donors fund rebuilding and reform efforts, social norms are in a state of flux, and the political climate may be conducive to change (Percival et al. 2014). This reform period presents favourable circumstances for the promotion of gender equity in multiple social arenas, including the health system (ibid.).

Valuing unpaid care work obviously contributes to gender equality, facilitates the equitable sharing of care work responsibilities, and contributes to social equity (Rubery 2015). Porter (2003: 246) cites that the United Nations understands gender equality as "a goal to ensure equal rights, responsibilities and opportunities of women and men, and girls and boys". Gender equality (recognition of unpaid care work and domestic work) is increasingly becoming a top policy priority through strengthened international commitments—the Sustainable Development Goals 2030. At present, gender is a dimension that is routinely added on as a component to most programs, partly because international agencies have come to insist on its inclusion (Ibnouf 2013). Brimblecombe et al. (2018) posit that reconciliation of unpaid care and employment is thus an increasingly important societal, economic, and equality issue. Women's literacy, girls' education, and a more equitable balance of care work are needed to improve women's status (Marphatia and Moussié 2013).

Gender inequality, in society, stems from the unequal division of paid work outside the family and of unpaid work within the family (Lewis 2009). UN Women (2012)[2] states that only 7% of agreements signed between 1990 and 2010 referenced gender equality or/and women's rights. World Bank distinguishes equality under the law, equality of opportunity (equality of rewards for work and equality in access to human capital and other productive resources that enable opportunity), and equality of voice (Bouta et al. 2005). It is likely that without a clear gender equality focus, interventions will fail to capitalize on opportunities to decrease disparities between women and men and to build on their potential to sustain peace (Bouta et al. 2005).

The main point feminists have stress on about gender equality is the perception that society holds about the attainment of gender equality through care work, revealing that the disproportionate burden of unpaid care work on women limits their rights and opportunities, which is a major determinant of gender inequality (Folbre 2006). Women need to be given a proactive working environment that supports them in delivering their best. The equal sharing of care work responsibilities between women and men needs to be taken very seriously—that is equality in true sense. States must adopt policy making measures in view of care work, to ensure that social and economic policies across all areas are promoting a fair sharing of care work responsibilities between women and men, in the short, medium and long term (UN 2013). Equal sharing is more plausible combined with a high de-familiarization of care (Rubery 2015) to attain gender equality.

Gender equality relates to the equal rights, responsibilities, and opportunities of women, men, girls, and boys (Bouta et al. 2005). In 2009, the Africa Union Summit held in Addis Ababa declared 2010–2020 as the African Women's Decade (AWD), which is being organized under the theme "Grassroots Approach to Gender Equality and Women's Empowerment". Gender equality forms part of the national policy agenda, yet daunting realities displaced women are facing are still barely addressed. Most African countries have adopted national laws on gender equality, implementing budgets with a gender perspective and mainstreaming gender in planning systems. While there are so many instruments expressing the formal commitments of African governments to the agenda of gender equality, translating these theoretical promises into concrete action remains a formidable challenge (Olowu 2011). Undervaluation of care work by women and lack of consideration of their needs and interests, at macro- and micro-levels, have undermined their enjoyment of the benefits of gender equality in post-conflict.

National capacity building in the immediate post-conflict situation is often approached as a gender-neutral measure. It is assumed that women benefit as much as men from "gender-neutral" investment, aid management, and the revival of public services. Without paying much attention to women's caregiving responsibilities, social policies serve to disable caregivers and maintain gendered care work rather than to challenge the unequal delegation of care work responsibilities. Appropriate supportive services such as childcare centres, literacy classes, saving-led micro-finance, micro-enterprises, and flexitime jobs are not available or affordable to displaced women, which are also essential to promoting gender equality. Unpaid care work is identified as one of the four important areas where progress would substantially reduce gender inequalities, other three being education, financial and digital inclusion, and legal protection (Woetzel 2015 cited in Narayan 2017: 654).

The commitment to gender equality in development responses rests on the belief that human development should promote an environment in which both women and men can develop their full potential through the strengthening of human capabilities. Sad but true—human rights arguments are often not enough to achieve change in communities that are very patriarchal. Thus, the quest for gender equality needs multi-pronged approaches at one hand, and on the other hand it needs a continuous policy advocacy with the legislators and the decision makers so as to bring some positive legislation on these issues. Care is at the heart of debates on how we reproduce society (Raghuram 2016). Post-conflict settings create potential environments for positive change for women and could contribute to important societal changes that can be important for policy making. It can be concluded that gender equality and women empowerment remain as paramount contributors to the stability of post-armed conflict communities.

The main problem feminist activism face is how to sensitize women about their rights and gender equality. Women's rights acknowledgement is not just concerning women, but it helps in widening the very concept of justice upon which the international human rights' system is based. It makes the concept of justice to be an inclusive one. Recognition of the possibilities of inequality within caring relationships draws attention to the needs of policy to respond in a way which does not place too much of a burden on the women as caregivers (Clough 2015). Reforming policy during or immediately in the wake of "crisis", such as war, is much easier than during "normal" times, when policies are entrenched. The state should seize these ideal opportunities to reduce gender inequality. Concrete actions (i.e. gender sensitive policies and laws) should be taken when these opportunities arise. Legal reforms from a gender perspective which means that laws and regulations should incorporate international standards and commitments, which guarantees fundamental human rights and equality of men and women in access to political, economic, and social aspects of life, should be implemented. This may require lobbying and moral suasion.

Notes

1. Leaving no one behind is a fundamental tenet of the 2030 Sustainable Development Goal (SDG) agenda, agreed in September 2015. The 2030 Sustainable Development Goal https://www.un.org/sustainabledevelopment/sustainable-development-goals/.
2. UN Women. "Women's Participation in Peace Negotiations: Connections Between Presence and Influence", October 2012, p. 3.

Bibliography

Adeogun, T.J., and J.M. Muthuki. 2017. "Only the Person Who Wears the Shoes Knows Where the Shoes Pinch": Reworking Bottom-Up Approach in South Sudan. *Women's Studies International Forum* 62 (1): 83–90.

Adeogun, T.J., and J.M. Muthuki. 2018. Feminist Perspectives on Peacebuilding: The Case of Women's Organizations in South Sudan. *Agenda* 32 (2): 1–10.

Alaga, E. 2010. Challenges for Women in Peacebuilding in West Africa. Africa Institute of South Africa, Policy Briefs, AISA, June 2010, No. 18: 1–9.

Arostegui, J. 2013. Gender, Armed Conflict, and Peace-Building: How Armed Conflict Can Catalyze Positive Change for Women. *Gender & Development* 21 (3): 533–549. Published Online 11 November 2013. http://dx.doi.org/10.1080/13552074.2013.846624.

Barash, D., and C.P. Webel. 2009. *Peace and Conflict Studies*, 2nd ed. Thousand Oaks, CA: Sage.

Bell, C., C. Campbell, and F.N. Aoláin. 2004. Justice Discourses in Transition. *Social and Legal Studies* 13 (3): 305–328.

Bendaña, A. 2003. What Kind of Peace Is Being Built? Critical Assessments from the South. Paper for the International Development Research Centre, Ottawa, Canada, January 2003.

Björnberg, K. 2012. *Rethinking Human Security: Taking into Consideration Based Violence*. Stellenbosch: Stellenbosch University.

Bouta, T., G. Frerks, and I. Bannon. 2005. *Gender, Conflict, and Development*. Washington, DC: World Bank.

Brimblecombe, N., J. Fernandez, M. Knapp, A. Rehill, and R. Wittenberg. 2018. Review of the International Evidence on Support for Unpaid Carers. *Journal of Long-Term Care*, 25–40. Published Online 1 September 2018. https://doi.org/10.21953/lse.ffq4txr2nftf.

Brock-Utne, B. 1990. Feminist Perspectives on Peace. In *A Reader in Peace Studies*, ed. P. Smoker, R. Davies, and B. Munske, 144–150. New York: Pergamon Press.

Brück, T., and K. Schindler. 2008. The Impact of Conflict and Fragility on Households a Conceptual Framework with Reference to Widows. Research Paper No. 2008/83, UNU World Institute for Development Economics Research (UNU-WIDER).

Brück, T., and M. Vothknecht. 2011. Impact of Violent Conflicts on Women's Economic Opportunities. In: *Women and War: Power and Protection in the 21st Century*, eds. K. Kuehnast, C. de Jonge Oudraat, and H. Hernes, 85–114. Washington, DC: United States Institute of Peace Press.

Busumtwi-Sam, J. 2008. Contextualizing Human Security: A 'Deprivation–Vulnerability' Approach. *Policy and Society* 27 (1): 15–28. Published Online 3 March 2017. https://doi.org/10.1016/j.polsoc.2008.07.002.

Carroll, B. 1987. Feminism and Pacifism: Historical and Theoretical Connections. In *Women and Peace: Theoretical, Historical and Practical Perspectives*, ed. Ruth Roach Pierson, 2–28. London: Croom Helm.

Clough, B. 2015. Exploring the Potential of Relational Approaches to Mental Capacity Law. PhD Thesis, University of Manchester, Faculty of Humanities, Manchester.

Confortini, C.C. 2010. Feminist Contributions and Challenges to Peace Studies. International Studies Association Compendium.

De Coning, C. 2018. Adaptive Peacebuilding. *International Affairs* 94 (2): 301–317. Published by Oxford University Press on Behalf of The Royal Institute of International Affairs. https://doi.org/10.1093/ia/iix251.

Dyck, I. 2005. Feminist Geography, the 'Everyday', and Local-Global Relations: Hidden Spaces of Place-Making. *Canadian Geographer/Le Géographe canadien* 49 (3): 233–243. Published Online September 2005. https://doi.org/10.1111/j.0008-3658.2005.00092.x.

Engle, P.L., P. Menon, and L. Haddad. 1999. Care and Nutrition: Concepts and Measurement. *World Development* 27 (8): 1309–1337.

Erzurum, K., and B. Eren. 2014. Women in Peacebuilding: A Criticism of Gendered Solutions in Post-conflict Situations. *Journal of Applied Security Research* 9 (2): 236–256. Published Online April 2014. https://doi.org/10.1080/19361610.2014.883297.

Esplen, E. 2009. *Gender and Care: An Overview Report*. Brighton: BRIDGE/IDS. http://www.bridge.ids.ac.uk/reports/cep_care_or.pdf.

Ferrant, G., L.M. Pesando, and K. Nowacka. 2014. Unpaid Care Work: The Missing Link in the Analysis of Gender Gaps in Labor Outcomes. Issue Paper, OECD Development Center.

Folbre, N. 2006. Measuring Care: Gender, Empowerment, and the Care Economy. *Journal of Human Development* 7 (2): 183–199. Published Online 22 January 2007. https://doi.org/10.1080/14649880600768512.

Folbre, N., and J.A. Nelson. 2000. For Love or Money—Or Both? *Journal of Economic Perspectives* 14 (4): 123–140.

Gasper, D., and T. Truong. 2008. Development Ethics Through the Lenses of Caring, Gender, and Human Security. Working Paper, No. 459, Institute of Social Studies, Netherlands.

Gasper, D., L.J.G. van der Maesen, T. Truong, and A. Walker. 2008. Human Security and Social Quality: Contrasts and Complementarities. Working Paper, No. 462, Institute of Social Studies, Netherlands.

Gheaus, A. 2012. Gender Justice. *Journal of Ethics and Social Philosophy* 6 (2): 1–24.

Gilligan, C. 1982. *In a Different Voice: Psychological Theory and Women's Development*. Boston and Cambridge, MA: Harvard University Press.

Grasa, R., and O. Mateos. 2010. Conflict, Peace and Security in Africa: An Assessment and New Questions After 50 Years of African Independence. Institut Catala Internacional (ICIP), Working Papers 2010/08.

Green, B. 2012. Applying Feminist Ethics of Care to Nursing Practice. *Journal of Nursing and Care* 1 (3): 1–4. Published online January 2012. https://doi.org/10.4172/2167-1168.1000111.

Guttieri, K., and J. Piombo. 2007. *Interim Governments: Institutional Bridges to Peace and Democracy?* Washington, DC: United States Institute of Peace.

Haeri, M., and N. Puechguirbal. 2010. From Helplessness to Agency: Examining the Plurality of Women's Experiences in Armed Conflict. *International Review of the Red Cross* 92 (877): 103–122.

Hirway, I. 2015. Unpaid Work and the Economy: Linkages and Their Implications. *Indian Journal of Labour Economics* 58 (1): 1–21. Published Online December 2015. https://doi.org/10.1007/s41027-015-0010-3.

Hudson, H. 2009. Peacebuilding Through a Gender Lens and the Challenges of Implementation in Rwanda and Côte d'Ivoire. *Security Studies* 18 (2): 287–318.

Ibnouf, F.O. 2013. Women and the Arab Spring Revolutions: Is There a Window of Opportunity or Can We Expect More of the Same? Published in E-International Relations. http://www.e-ir.info/.

Jeong, H.W. 2005. *Peace Building in Post-Armed Conflict Societies: Processes and Strategies*. Boulder, CO and London: Lynne Rienner.

Karam, A. 2000. Women in War and Peace-Building: The Roads Traversed, the Challenges Ahead. *International Feminist Journal of Politics* 3 (1): 2–25.

Kingston, A.K. 2007. *Mothering Special Needs: A Different Maternal Journey*, 1st ed. London and Philadelphia: Jessica Kingsley.

Krause, J., W. Krause, and P. Bränfors. 2018. Women's Participation in Peace Negotiations and the Durability of Peace. *International Interactions* 44 (6): 985–1016. Published Online 10 August 2018. https://doi.org/10.1080/03050629.2018.1492386.

Lewis, J. 2009. *Work-Family Balance, Gender and Policy.* Cheltenham, UK: Edward Elgar.

Liamputtong, P. 2011. *Focus Group Methodology Principle and Practice*, 1st ed. Thousand Oaks: Sage.

Linsley, P.M. 2017. Application of an Ethic of Care to Business. In *Handbook of Virtue Ethics in Business and Management*, ed. A. Sison, G. Beabout, and I. Ferrero. International Handbooks in Business Ethics. Dordrecht: Springer.

Lloyd, L. 2006. A Caring Profession? The Ethics of Care and Social Work with Older People. *British Journal of Social Work* 36: 1171–1185. Published online November 2005. https://doi.org/10.1093/bjsw/bch400.

Maestre, M., and J. Thorpe. 2016, May. *Understanding Unpaid Care Work to Empower Women in Market Systems Approaches.* London: The BEAM Exchange. Retrieved from https://www.beamexchange.org.

Mahon, R., and F. Robinson. 2011. *Feminist Ethics and Social Policy Towards a New Global Political Economy of Care.* Vancouver: UBC Press.

Manchanda, R. 2005. Women's Agency in Peace Building: Gender Relations in Post-conflict Reconstruction. *Economic and Political Weekly* 40 (44/45): 4737–4745.

Manchanda, R. 2004. Gender Conflict and Displacement: Contesting 'Infantilisation' of Forced Migrant Women. *Economic and Political Weekly* 39 (37): 4179–4186.

Mangena, F. 2009. The Search for an African Feminist Ethic: A Zimbabwean Perspective. *Journal of International Women's Studies* 11 (2): 18–30.

Marphatia, A.A., and R. Moussié. 2013. A Question of Gender Justice: Exploring the Linkages Between Women's Unpaid Care Work, Education, and Gender Equality. *International Journal of Educational Development* 33: 585–594. Published Online November 2013. https://doi.org/10.1016/j.ijedudev.2013.05.005.

McCarthy, L. 2018. "There Is No Time for Rest": Gendered CSR, Sustainable Development and the Unpaid Care Work Governance Gap. *Business Ethics: A European Review* 27 (4): 337–349. Published Online 27 September 2018. https://doi.org/10.1111/beer.12190.

McKenzie, J.A. 2016. An Exploration of an Ethics of Care in Relation to People with Intellectual Disability and Their Family Caregivers in the Cape Town Metro-Pole in South Africa. *ALTER—European Journal of Disability Research* 10 (1): 67–78.

Metz, T., and J.B.R. Gaie. 2010. The African Ethic of Ubuntu/Botho: Implications for Research on Morality. *Journal of Moral Education* 39 (3): 273–290.

Moussié, R., and L. Alfers. 2016. Women Informal Workers Demand Child Care: Shifting Narratives on Women's Economic Empowerment in Africa. *Agenda* 32 (1): 119–131.

Narayan, N. 2017. Contextualizing Unpaid Care Work and Women Empowerment. *International Journal of Applied Research* 3 (7): 654–659.

Nelson, J.A. 2011. Care Ethics and Markets: A View from Feminist Economics. In *Applying Care Ethics to Business*, ed. M. Hamington and M. Sander-Staudt. Dordrecht: Springer.

Netabay, N. 2009. The Darfur Peace Process: Understanding the Obstacles to Success. M.A. Thesis, University Notre Dame, Indiana.

Neufeldt, R.C. 2017. *Ethics of Peacebuilding*. Oxford: Oxford Research Encyclopedias, International Studies Association and Oxford University Press.

Olowu, D. 2011. Mainstreaming Women, Equating Men: Charting an Inclusionary Approach to Transformative Development in the African Decade for Women. *Law, Democracy & Development* 15: 1–22. https://doi.org/10.4314/ldd.v15i1.2.

Orozco, A.P. 2009. Global Perspectives on the Social Organization of Care in Times of Crisis: Assessing the Situation. Working Paper 5: Gender, Migration and Development Series, United Nations International Research and Training, Institute for the Advancement of Women (INSTRAW).

O'Reilly, M., A.Ó. Súilleabháin, and T. Paffenholz. 2015. *Reimagining Peacemaking: Women's Roles in Peace Processes*. New York: International Peace Institute.

Pankhurst, D. 2003. The 'Sex War' and Other Wars: Towards a Feminist Approach to Peace Building. *Development in Practice* 13 (2): 154–177.

Parmar, P.K., P. Agrawal, R. Goyal, J. Scott, and P.G. Greenough. 2014. Need for a Gender-Sensitive Human Security Framework: Results of a Quantitative Study of Human Security and Sexual Violence in Djohong District, Cameroon. *Conflict and Health* 8 (6): 1–12. Published Online 7 May 2014. https://doi.org/10.1186/1752-1505-8-6.

Percival, V., E. Richards, T. MacLean, and S. Theobald. 2014. Health Systems and Gender in Post-Armed Conflict Contexts: Building Back Better? *Conflict and Health* 8 (19): 1–14. Published Online October 2014. https://doi.org/10.1186/1752-1505-8-19.

Piergallini, I. 2014. *Is the Path Towards a 'Caring Economy' Possible? Care Work from Personal Service to Collective Responsibility*. Venice: Università Ca' Foscari Venezia.

Pitanguy, J. 2011. Reconceptualizing Peace and Violence Against Women: A Work in Progress. *Signs* 36 (3): 561–566.

Porter, E. 2003. Women, Political Decision-Making, and Peace-Building. *Global Change, Peace & Security* 15 (3): 245–262. Published Online October 2003. https://doi.org/10.1080/0951274032000124965.

Porter, E. 2008. Review: Why Women's Contribution to Peacebuilding Matters. *International Studies Review* 10 (3): 632–634.

Powell, C. 2017. How Women Could Save the World, If Only We Would Let Them: From Gender Essentialism to Inclusive Security. *Yale Journal of Law & Feminism* 28 (2): 272–325.

Raghuram, P. 2016. Locating Care Ethics Beyond the Global North. *ACME: An International Journal of Critical Geographies* 15 (3): 511–533.

Rahele, A. 2016. Explaining and Critique of Feminisms' Ethical (Moral) Philosophy. *International Journal of Humanities and Cultural Studies (IJHCS)*. Special Issue, 2266–2281. ISSN 2356-5926.

Rao, N. 2018. Global Agendas, Local Norms: Mobilizing Around Unpaid Care and Domestic Work in Asia. *Development and Change* 49 (3): 735–758.

Razavi, S. 2007. The Political and Social Economy of Care in a Development Context: Conceptual Issues, Research Questions and Policy Options. Gender and Development, Paper No. 3, UNRISD, Geneva.

Remenyi, K. 2016. Does the Inclusion of Women in Peace Building Processes Make a Difference? E-International Relations. https://www.e-ir.info.

Robinson, F. 2011. *The Ethics of Care: A Feminist Approach to Human Security.* Philadelphia: Temple University Press.

Rubery, J. 2015. Regulating for Gender Equality: A Policy Framework to Support the Universal Caregiver Vision. *Social Politics* 22 (4): 513–538.

Rummery, K., and M. Fine. 2012. Care: A Critical Review of Theory, Policy and Practice. *Social Policy & Administration* 46 (3): 321–343. Published Online June 2012. https://doi.org/10.1111/j.1467-9515.2012.00845.x.

Santa-Barbara, J. 2007. Reconciliation. In *Handbook of Peace and Armed Conflict Studies*, ed. C. Webel and J. Galtung, 173–186. Routledge: London.

Schmidt, E.M. 2018. Breadwinning as Care? The Meaning of Paid Work in Mothers' and Fathers' Constructions of Parenting. *Community, Work & Family* 21 (4): 445–462. Published Online April 2017. https://doi.org/10.1080/13668803.2017.1318112.

Seguino, S. 2011. Help or Hindrance? Religion's Impact on Gender Inequality in Attitudes and Outcomes. *World Development* 39 (8): 1308–1321.

Sharoni, S. 2010. Conflict Resolution: Feminist Perspectives. In *The International Studies Encyclopedia*, ed. R. Denemark. New York: Wiley-Blackwell.

Shulika, L.S., and L. Shulika. 2016. Women and Peace Building: From Historical to Contemporary African Perspectives. *Ubuntu: Journal of Conflict Transformation* 5 (1): 7–31.

Sidonia, A. 2018. *Women in Peacemaking and Peacebuilding in Northern Uganda*. Cham, Switzerland: Springer.
Sikod, Fo. 2007. Gender Division of Labour and Women's Decision-Making Power in Rural Households in Cameroon. *Africa Development* XXXII (3): 58–71. Council for the Development of Social Science Research in Africa (CODESRIA), Dakar.
Sjoberg, L. 2009. *Gender and International Security: Feminist Perspectives*, 1st ed. Series: Routledge Critical Security Studies. London: Routledge.
Smits, J. 2010. Ethnic Intermarriage and Social Cohesion: What Can We Learn from Yugoslavia? *Social Indicators Research* 96 (3): 417–432. Published Online May 2010. https://doi.org/10.1007/s11205-009-9485-y.
Stuart, E., K. Bird, T. Bhatkal, R. Greenhill, S. Lally, G. Rabinowitz, E. Samman, M.B. Sarwar, and A. Lynch. 2016. Leaving No One Behind: A Critical Path for the First 1,000 Days of the Sustainable Development Goals. Overseas Development Institute (ODI), Development Progress Flagship Report, London.
Tadesse, B., Y. Tesfaye, and F. Beyene. 2010. Women in Conflict and Indigenous Conflict Resolution Among the Issa and Gurgura Clans of Somali in Eastern Ethiopia. *African Journal on Conflict Resolution* 10 (1): 85–110.
UN Women. 2012, October. *Women's Participation in Peace Negotiations: Connections between Presence and Influence*, 2nd ed., 3. https://peaceoperationsreview.org/wpcontent/uploads/2015/11/womens_partcipation_peace.pdf.
UN—United Nations. 2013. Extreme Poverty and Human Rights: Unpaid Care Work and Women's Human Rights. Sepulveda Carmona, M. The Special Rapporteur's Report to the 68th Session of the General Assembly (A/68/293).
Walby, S. 2007. Complexity Theory, Systems Theory and Multiple Intersecting Social Inequalities. *Philosophy of the Social Sciences* 37 (4): 449–70. Sage.
Weiss, A.M. 2003. Interpreting Islam and Women's Rights: Implementing CEDAW in Pakistan. *International Sociology* 18 (3): 581–601. Published Online September 2003. https://doi.org/10.1177/02685809030183007.
Young, J. 2005. Sudan: A Flawed Peace Process Leading to a Flawed Peace. *Review of African Political Economy* 32 (103): 99–113.
Young, H., A.M. Osman, A.M. Abusin, M. Asher, and O. Egemi. 2009. Livelihoods, Power and Choice: The Vulnerability of the Northern Rizaygat, Darfur, Sudan. Feinstein International Center, Tufts University.
Zachorowska-Mazurkiewicz, A. 2015. The Concept of Care in Institutional and Feminist Economics and Its Impact on Public Policy. *Journal of Economic* 49 (2): 405–413.

CHAPTER 7

Lessening the Distance Between Peacebuilding and Ground Reality

7.1 Making Care Work Visible

Women play a vital role as caregivers for the survival and well-being of their families and communities in wartime. This work needs to be officially acknowledged and women should be given seats in peace negotiation tables. The interviewees in Darfur affirmed the importance of their role as caregivers and desired their roles be expanded to involve participating in formal peacebuilding processes and their bulk of unpaid care work lessened.

Women as caregivers are indispensable. The interviewed women as caregivers lamented—*We paid the price of war. We do not ask for anything in return because we do it for the peace of the whole nation.* Their time in wartime is "infinitely inelastic". They have to fulfil their care work responsibilities irrespective of whatever predicaments they may find themselves in. Needlessly, men are criticized for helping out in care work as it is considered "feminine work". Even when these women become job holders in post-conflict, their care workload remains the same. Policymakers and peace practitioners need to root for changing circumstances for these women.

The invisibility, unequal distribution and the extremely cumbersome nature of unpaid care works have a negative impact on women; the same conclusion was echoed in another study undertaken by Maestre and Thorpe (2016) who added time constraints, poverty, poor health and

F. O. Ibnouf, *War-Time Care Work and Peacebuilding in Africa*, Gender, Development and Social Change,
https://doi.org/10.1007/978-3-030-26195-5_7

well-being, limited mobility, and the perpetuation of women's unequal status in society. Making wartime care work "visible", would be particularly important for women as caregivers to raise their concerns. This is because care work during and after war is predominantly provided by women alone. Giving a voice to caregivers to express their views derived from their lived experiences maximizes their potentials as actors for peacebuilding. It would help in adopting policies for supporting unpaid care work in post-conflict situations, through the State, or by households with financial support from the state.

In IDP societies, girls are expected to stay at home and assist their mothers in performing care woks. This preoccupies them and prevents them from schooling or excelling in studies when schooling. Girls themselves may not see the value of education if the expectation remains that they will continue in their roles as caregivers (Dodson and Dickert 2004).

Practical experiences of women as care givers can be very useful in formal peacebuilding processes. Women as caregivers are often stereotyped as victims of war rather than as agents of peace. The burden of unpaid care work is one of the barriers that hinder women from fully participating in peacebuilding. The patriarchal structures have swayed women's narratives away from peace processes. Furthermore, these women need to be trained on formal peacebuilding tools adapted to their specific contexts.

Peace is based only on the perspectives of men and neglects the standpoints of women. A sustainable peace can be driven by women as caregivers. Care work is almost never recognized in peacebuilding negotiations, policies, and programs. This book proves the need to have women as caregivers participating at the peace table. This will benefit women as caregivers, make visible their contribution and participation towards survival and well-being of their societies, and the other half of the population will no longer be left behind. Diverse war experiences could be especially valuable when brought onto the negotiation table. It generates new insights and ideas and at the same time, helps to build a more comprehensive peace.

Care work contributes to peacebuilding because caregivers do not see themselves as victims but rather as survivors and then peacebuilders. They know that care breeds peace. The lived experience of women can be made visible by extension, encouraging, humanitarian, and peace building efforts to include women and women's perspectives in their work, which helps to promote an alternative paradigm that is based on social justice and human rights, and in turn helps to strengthen women's movements and other social and political movements that are based on these values (Thompson et al. 2007).

Oftentimes women regard themselves as caregivers/providers, nurturers, peacemakers, or the agent of peace. They are non-combatants. However, women are noticeably absent, or at best underrepresented in peacebuilding processes and post-conflict reconstructions. Krause et al. (2018) argued that including women directly in peace negotiations with a voice and influence is not only a matter of justice, but also of effectiveness, quality, and sustainability of peace and leads to better accord content and higher agreement implementation rates. The absence of women's participation in peacebuilding and reconstruction processes silence their voices on issues, such as their burden of caregiving, displacement, rape and sexual violence, healthcare and girls' education.

Visibility of wartime care work is much needed, but visibility alone is not lessening the burden of care work on women in the real sense. Women should not be the only ones in charge of care and peace building requires creating a comprehensive responsibility for care (men, governments, NGOs, INGOs, and CSOs should become co-responsible together with women). Recognition, reduction, and redistribution functions within the broader principle of care work would enable equal representation of women and men in peacebuilding and reconstruction processes. Compensation after war should involve the four principles of unpaid care work which are recognition, reduction, redistribution, and representation to be well-established in all social policies. Redistribution and recognition function within the broader framework of representation, enabling equal participation in social life (Fraser 2007). The UN High-Level Panel on Women's Economic Empowerment also identified these four principles (4 Rs) for addressing care deficits through policies and programs; these include the recognition, reduction, redistribution, and representation of unpaid care (United Nations 2017). Recognition can take several forms, including provision of compensation for the work, recognizing it when determining other benefits, such as pension payments, or measuring unpaid care work in national statistics (Budlender and Moussié 2013). This will allow for different perspectives to be heard, enriches the peacebuilding processes, and increases the relevance and engagement. Thus, making wartime care work visible includes various states of the procedure, viz. measures targeted specifically at caregivers, but do have important implications for integration of women in peacebuilding and post-conflict constructions. The recognition of the value of care work performed by women should be done by guaranteeing them a leading voice in peace building and by recognizing care at the heart of peace, and the redistribution of care responsibilities between all social actors and also within wider social institutions to bring about equal societies and sustainable peace. In terms of measures, there is a need for new measures developed specifically for caregivers as well as for the implications of general policies or institutions that may affect caregivers' integration. For instance, combination of appropriate policy interventions aim to reduce arduous care tasks through, for example, labour-saving equipment that can facilitate care and domestic activities and contribute to redistribute care responsibilities from women to the household, the community, and the state/or market (or a combination of these) by using a facilitation approach.

Unpaid care work represents an obstacle to women's access to the job market (paid work). Socialist feminists have always argued that to achieve equality in paid work, women also need to achieve equality in unpaid work (Elson 2017). The strategies that can help to achieve this can be summarized as "recognize, reduce, and redistribute" the burden of unpaid care work, which falls almost exclusively on women (ibid.). Krause et al. (2018) cited that gender equality has been shown to be a strong indicator of a state's peacefulness. It is a State's responsibility to develop effective social policies guided by using "feminist ethics of care" to ensure nothing has been left out and caregiving by women has been given priority. An effective strategic plan takes into account lessening caregivers' burden and providing caregivers with care needed supports and resources. The women surveyed reveal the state has a critical role to play, it can provide basic care support but it cannot provide love and emotional support. Care includes emotional support and is loaded with "moral overtones concerning both duty and love" (Esquivel 2014).

Undervaluation of women's care work and lack of consideration of their needs and interests, at macro- and micro-levels, have undermined women's enjoyment of benefits and status in post-conflict. Some policymakers and peacebuilders think enough has been said and done for integrating women's concerns in peacebuilding. Others argue that women's rights are not important, because during conflict, the priority is to save lives and after conflict, everyone has to pull together to rebuild society and avoid further social disruption. Recognizing and acknowledging the role of women in unpaid care work arrangements during wartime and acting upon their needs to address the increased care responsibilities brought upon by conflicts and wars can have far-reaching and more sustainable impacts on peacebuilding efforts. It would be a step forward towards answering questions in a more complex conflict situation.

Feminist theory across a number of disciplinary fields has made a significant contribution to the understanding of care and to the development of its policy and practice in a variety of societal contexts (Himmelweit and Plomien 2014: 446). Responsibility for ensuring that care work does not lead to poverty and social exclusion should be taken out of the private sphere and reframed as a collective responsibility. Under this renegotiated social contract, each individual engaging in care work would have a range of socio-economic rights met by the state, rather than by the family members (Lynch et al. 2009 cited in Zachorowska-Mazurkiewicz 2015). Engster states that the general duty to care thus entails a duty to organize collective caring institutions, such as governments, to meet basic needs, such as safety and security that individuals cannot meet alone (cited in Friedman 2009).

Caregivers' needs and priorities are disregarded in peace processes. They carry on care work for longer hours and are involved in more intensive and demanding activities during and after war. Arguably, the burden of unpaid care work means many women are simply not able to find time to realize their own right to education, health, or even decent paid work. The costs of providing care falls disproportionately on women and these costs include forgone opportunities in education, employment and earnings, political participation, and leisure time (Esquivel 2013). Women as caregivers need to be represented from the very first stages of the peacebuilding process. Considering women as caregivers in a way that satisfies their needs is an essential step towards lasting peace. The Global Gender Gap Report (GGGR) 2015[1] reported strong and persistent investment in women reaps considerable social and economic returns and this in turn has implications for the sustainability of peace. There is a need for an alternative human rights approach, which respects women's right to health, education, and simply put, to life.

Empowering women in conflict situations would help prevent gender-based violence such as the terrible crimes of rape, forced pregnancy, sexual slavery, and others (Naraghi-Anderlini 2006). Although they are in urgent need of psychological and physical care to help them to heal from their trauma and injuries, however, rape victims are the only caregivers for a child born as a result of rape. Women may be forced to care for such a child without assistance from even their close family members.

In Darfur, unpaid care work is the heart of the community with women as caregivers substituting government authorities in offering food and security to the needy. Notwithstanding the crucial role of women as caregivers during wartime and their role in informal peace building, however women have been excluded from peace negotiations. Furthermore, most post-armed conflict planning for reconstruction continues to ignore or inadequately account for caregiving issues. The local ownership of the peace processes is of course of monumental importance. The post-conflict program and policy need to be part of a holistic approach, one that views men and women as actors of change and instrumental to the country's reconstruction process. Moreover, for any overall peacebuilding process to be meaningful, it needs to be firmly grounded in the reality. This ensures pragmatic solutions to peacebuilding. Finally, no war/conflict has been resolved by military force. Care work is one of the ways that can neutralize violence.

7.2 The Social and Public Policies Fall Way Short of Even the Basics

The question rises whether policies (social, welfare, etc.) adequately address women as caregivers' priorities and needs, particularly in conflict contexts. Currently, social protection services and policies that serve to alleviate the effects of the unequal distribution of tasks continue to be inadequate, especially in countries in which there are privations of the magnitude of those in Africa (Domínguez-Serrano 2012). This removes the possibility that these services can be covered by the paid private sector, thus transferring most of the responsibility for the welfare of dependent people to the home environment (ibid.). According to a report by United Nations Population Fund (UNFPA 2001), the essential services such as basic health care, including reproductive health care and counselling, are often disrupted or inaccessible during conflict. This presents health risks for all affected populations, at times when public health needs soar.

In post-armed conflict situations, little has been done to so address care challenges already at hand. The burden of care will remain entirely and unfairly on the shoulders of women, if the government and associated care-providers institutions abdicate their responsibilities. The care provided by care public services is much lower than what is needed. During and after war, there are no services, which would provide relief to caregivers burdened with care work. Women as caregivers with high care burden lack access to appropriate and affordable technologies to ease their work of household duties and relieving their time constraints. Domestic support technologies and basic social infrastructure are not commonly available, which make housekeeping chores such as fetching water, collecting firewood, and food processing absorb a great deal of time for women and girls. The formal care services are unable to keep up with increasing demand for such services in post-conflict setting. This pressure is expected to increase considerably in the future due to epidemic diseases and conflict trauma.

Women are care providers but are also care demanders. When the role of women in wartime care work is ignored or side-lined, women are denied their basic rights, such as reproductive health right. Among the ten countries with the highest risk of maternal death, are some African countries most of which are at war today or are in a post-conflict situation, including Sierra Leone, Chad, Angola, Liberia, Somalia, and the Democratic Republic of the Congo (Landers 2009). Maternal mortality is still at a staggeringly high rate in women living in war-affected areas in Darfur. The study conducted by Haggaz et al. (2007: 252) to investigate the incidence and causes of maternal deaths in Darfur found high maternal mortality, which is expected to increase in this region because of the ongoing conflict and the epidemic of contagious diseases such as viral hepatitis. This might be attributed to the lack of working health centres meaning an unknown number had died at home in childbirth. In fact, in Darfur deliveries in the IDP camps are usually attended to by the traditional birth attendants because they are affordable. Maternal health and family planning are still unknown concepts for so many girls and women as Darfur case shows. Culture devalues family planning because having many children is sometimes seen as a point of pride and respect. Reproductive health and rights should be integrated as an essential agenda in the peace talks. Sexual violence and abuses, maternal health care and girls' education, among others alike are shrivelled in peace processes and reconstruction efforts, and provided inadequate funding.

Despite real and significant needs, the realization of women's human rights has not been made a benchmark of success in post-conflict services, which tend to have poor female representation. There has already been some legalization for gender war-based violence, but still mechanisms for enforcement needs to be put in place. Many challenges still persist regarding violence against women in and out war. Conditions in the IDP camps are usually bleak and allow violence against women to thrive. The policymakers and judicial systems have to work together to put and invoke human rights legal mechanisms based on UNSCR 1888 to bring justice and to remove obstacles blocking these victims of violence/rape to access legal and judicial services through Africa. Without such effective legal mechanisms that incriminate all kinds of violence, it is almost impossible to see any change because unless the perpetrators face dire consequences for their acts, they will never feel a need to stop aggressing women at household or in their society. Without legal and judicial structures in place, women themselves can be at risk of imprisonment if they report violence.

The government was failed so far to take appropriate measures to ensure that the necessary health-care services and facilities are adequately available. Health care should be made accessible to IDPs by means acceptable to them, through their full participation and at a cost that all can afford. It involves managing health care concerns within the broader social determinants of health to ensure the affected population gets the best healthcare possible. NGOs and humanitarian programs tend to focus on life-saving operations and reproductive healthcare is generally not deemed a priority. Most international non-governmental organizations (INGOs) programs are usually ad hoc, very short, and they do not consider women as caregivers. Unfortunately, INGOs, NGOs, and civil society organizations (CSOs) have not been able to work in harmony as there is always mistrust and arguments on priority areas—as indicated by displaced women during focus group discussions. In addition, government officials have always felt that the INGOs, NGOs, and CSOs work with the opposition and have different agendas.

At present most IDPs camps' health centres are understaffed and under-resourced. The problem is the shortage of the health personnel, limited supply of drugs, and also the healthcare units and dressing units are in bad condition. Moreover, most IDPs' basic services are staffed by volunteer providers, nurses, teachers, midwives, etc. In improving maternal health, all women need access to antenatal care in pregnancy, skilled care during childbirth, and care and support in the weeks after childbirth. There is a need for public health antenatal care for provision of safer delivery and the immunization services of children. Unpaid care work would be reduced if key services were provided closer to where people live and work so that less time is spent accessing healthcare and education (Budlender and Moussié 2013). However, the question is whether such basic services could create sufficient well-being to the IDPs.

Despite the existence of resolution 1325—and the adoption of important follow-up resolutions in 2008 and 2009—it has been a persistent failure to seriously address gender equality issues and empower women in many African armed conflict and post-armed conflict situations. There are two key challenges in ensuring the effective inclusion of gender equality (including care work issues) within women, peace, and security concerns. First, there is a need for institutions which are sensitive to gender issues, and committed to promoting gender equality as a part of post-armed conflict reconstruction processes. Second, women's full participation in these institutions needs to be supported through capacity building and awareness raising programs. Useful indicators and outcomes that should form part of a successful UNSCR 1325; one example would be the gender dimension of the unpaid care work. For instance, what are the differing roles of women and men pertaining to unpaid care work during and after war? How can the priorities and needs of caregivers/providers be met by the various institutions and related actors? After having decided on some benchmarks, how can they be quantified in a way that can give an idea of a meaningful progress in the post-armed conflict situations? The idea is that the integration of wartime care work would only become a concern once a status of caregivers has been granted. How can these suggestions work out in practice?

7.3 Policy Relevance—How the True Need Can Be Changed into Actions?

Nowadays "care is becoming a more and more burning policy issue in almost every society" (Kröger 2009: 399). The role of governments in providing welfare and reducing the care load is crucial (Razavi 2007). Policies are needed to address the various constraints that disproportionately affect women as caregivers socially, healthily, and economically (access to paid-work opportunities). Social opportunities, in the form of education and health facilities, are meant to provide people with the capacity that they need to effectively shape their own destiny and help each other (Sen 1999: 11). Women play a vital role in wartime care work arrangement at their own personal risk and with very limited resources, to support survivors. Women's care role in the house gives priority to gender but have delegated domestic and care work to less privileged women. Women's socially acceptable roles are not regarded as issues that could or should be challenged while women constantly express dissatisfaction over difficulties arising from triple care work roles during and after war. They, therefore, desire greater male involvement in care work at the household level. Women do not want to jettison their unpaid care work roles. They are looking for family support and public facilities to enable them to perform their care roles more efficiently.

A number of general policy implications can be derived from the findings of this case study in Darfur. Women who provide unpaid care in and out of conflict need support services to be in place that enable the sharing of the care "burden". The support can be provided through the construction of the required appropriate infrastructure that alleviates unpaid care work burdens. It makes sense for the war-affected population to own the peacebuilding processes, especially women as caregivers. Caregivers need to be supported for their caring efforts, not discouraged, devalued, and belittled. Unpaid care work is both valuable and productive which requires investment in infrastructure to support caregivers/providers. States must adopt a care work approach in policy making, to ensure social and economic policies across all areas are promoting the better sharing of care between women and men, in the short, medium, and long term (UN 2013). Appropriate technologies will relieve care providers of a major burden that will help them go out into the work world with a stress-free and highly renewed vigour and will be able to see the opportunities therein from a wider and clearer perspective.

When people lack basic care and support, it can potentially become a barrier to effective peaceful life. Displaced camps around Africa need multidisciplinary services. The right to care should be introduced in the post-armed conflict reconstruction strategy and this should be linked to the goal of recognizing and supporting women as caregivers. Policies must be strengthened by a commitment to action if they are to be effective. There is a need to make the arrangement of caregiving an entry point of social and public policies and attendant practices directed for post-armed conflict communities. These changes can be translated into concrete improvements in the everyday lives of women and their families and into their rights and entitlements as women, as caregivers within the reconstruction planning. The social policies that do not relieve women's unpaid care-burden serve to reinforce gendered care and cultural injustice, with women being burdened by the care work role. Ensuring reliable, affordable, and easy access to basic services is crucial in alleviating the burden women often shoulder in obtaining healthcare, education, water, and food.

Wartime care work arrangement needs a more explicit debate on where the responsibilities of the state and families start and stop. Improving access for women to education so that they may develop the skills, knowledge, and self-confidence necessary to be active participants in reconstructions processes is of great importance. Without education, women as caregivers/providers access to understanding of the many challenges surrounding all aspects of their lives in post-conflict stage remains limited. These limitations will be a persistent drag on empowering women or attaining gender equality in all other aspects of theirlives. Connecting the national social policies to caregivers/providers' priorities and needs help in reducing the burden of unpaid care work. This may be done through appropriate time-saving technologies and basic services that would ease women heavy care workload. The cost of electricity is expensive for any rural region in Africa, let alone war and poverty ravaged areas. There is a need for renewable energy sources to reduce the cost of energy with security being an issue the need for more creatively solar as well as wind are in many ways more feasible to meet local energy needs in the African conflict context than electricity. Appropriate time-saving technologies will relieve caregivers of a major burden that will help them join the work force with a stress-free and highly renewed vigour and be able to see the opportunities therein from a wider and clearer perspective. Introduce simple, cost-effective ways of saving time in the home, such as energy-saving stoves, solar cookers that use the sun's rays will help in shortening the process of food cooking and reducing the need for daily firewood collection. Building the skills of women in areas of food processing and sewing would contribute to ease women's unpaid care work in home and open-up income-generating opportunities. Tanzania study shows according to Fälth and Blackden (2009), a one-hour reduction in fuel and water collection would increase by 7% the probability that women would engage in off-farm business activities.

The aftermath of war interventions is usually focused on collecting weapons from the armed groups and how former combatants can be reintegrated into society, and how displaced people can return to their homes. The implementation of the UNSCR 1325 is still lagging meaningful measures to address full engagement of women in peace negotiations, and in post-conflict reconstructions. Focusing on interventions in which the local people who experienced the conflict have a role to play is the best approach. Care work needs to be addressed by targeted interventions which require political will from the highest levels of the state. More flexibly and relevantly, programs and projects are needed in a manner tailored to the specific post-conflict stage and adapted to the needs and priorities of the target IDP population. Displaced people, both men and women, would immensely benefit if the state could consider basic care services to be a priority and increase healthcare investment. The women as caregivers have not had access to resources, credits, and other opportunities. None of the women respondents got credit from financial institutions as reported. Study by Morrison et al. (2007) indicates the existence of structural socio-economic barriers on women's ability to access services, and education often add more time pressure on the complex care workload on women. For Zuckerman and Greenberg (2004: 70), three interrelated kinds of rights which must be guaranteed to women in the post-conflict period are the right to participate meaningfully in policy making and resource allocation; the right to benefit equally from public and private resources and services; and the right to build a gender-equitable society for lasting peace and prosperity.

Post-armed conflict situation (weak and/or collapsed institutions, continuous insecurity etc.) has particular needs which need to be met to a certain degree. Integrating women in peace and security issues will help to strengthen the local, national, and regional governorship and the implementation of UNSCR 1325. Capacity building programs with a gender sensitive approach as well as a strong monitoring system are needed to successfully implement post-conflict reconstruction strategies. There is also a need to increase women's participation at all levels in society and a need to adopt a gender perspective on all aspects of the reconstruction and peacebuilding process. Women as caregivers and breadwinners at the grassroots level (those who live in the IDPs camps are mostly women) need to be continuously provided with capacity building to better equip them for actions at the ground level.

Collecting firewood, water, and cooking and processing of food products are physically demanding and time-consuming tasks. Such demands on caregivers force them to undertake excessive work, with potentially high health and well-being costs. Water security will enable women and girls to access drinking water close to home, alleviating their drudgery and the associated problems. A study from Tanzania indicates that reducing the time burdens of women could increase household cash incomes for smallholder farmers by 10% and labour productivity by 15% (Akinboade 2005: 259).

While men return home with anger, fear, and domination, women are less likely to accept their subordination after they have experienced relative autonomy and respect, which results in increased violence against women during peace times (Alaga 2010). It is not always religion, nor culture and tradition; rather it is power. The invisibility of sexual and rape problems is due to the lack of statistics, which creates difficulties not only in adopting laws for combating such violence, but also in changing social and cultural norms regarding this issue. The first steps in addressing this problem should be the development and adoption of effective statistical mechanisms that could measure rape in conflict situations. Woman/girl are all the time afraid from disclosing information about the rape incident, and that is due to the fear of being stigmatized, because she will not be tolerated neither by her family nor by the society and the environment where she lives in. She is always a “blamed victim”. The international community should not sit back and treat this as a matter within the domestic jurisdiction of the African community. Changing people’s attitudes is difficult; however, those who are in power bear the responsibility for leading the way. CSOs should take up the call for that law to discard immediately. Violence against women is indeed costly, “cost” is multi-dimensional. The victims often try to contain their pain, a lot of mental cases result from such bottled-up emotions.

In IDPs camps everywhere in Africa, there are more women than men, which should mean that if women are supported, there should be many women representing in post-conflict construction plans, simply by their numbers. Women rights which is rhetorically stated (at international women’s day, etc.) is not transferred in real or practical ways of dealing with women’s health, especially with regard to the facilities, the opportunities for counselling, preventative measures of violence against women. In practice, the enjoyment of human rights remains elusive for the majority of African women as caregivers. This situation is further compounded by low literacy rates and the lack of properly articulated laws that give legal basis for some discriminatory practices. Women’s socio-economic status must be strengthened. In addition, basic care services often neglected in terms of government response to appropriate measures and mechanisms is one significant concern that must be prioritized as it affects war-affected population and the sustainability of peacebuilding efforts in general.

The current administration of the IDP camps is represented in a combination of traditional and hierarchy-based social models. There are several actors and interactions. The Sheikh (traditional leader) is still the camp leader in the IDPs and always plays a central role between official authorities and humanitarian organizations and UNAMID.[2] Men are still playing leadership roles in the structures created in the IDP camps. Especially in the displaced camps, community leaders become the unavoidable link between the Darfurian population and international aid operations (Tubiana et al. 2012). Nonetheless, in displacement settings the demographic transition due to the absence of men (in battlefield) and increasing numbers of women, the crucial role of women in unpaid care becomes more visible to the humanitarian organizations. The surveyed sample reported that for the first time women are interacting with government institutions, CSOs and NGOs and humanitarian agencies. The need to go into public spaces to perform their care work made women to begin expanding their social networks and interacting with foreign and local actors or aid agencies (see also Berry 2018). How best can humanitarian and development agencies together with NGOs and CSOs link up caregiving arrangement and women capacity mechanisms to their overall humanitarian and development strategic frameworks in post-conflict settings?

The social and cultural structures are such that women are usually side-lined by men. Sevenhuijsen et al. (2003) suggest a responsive policy making framework that offers guidelines for a policy development process that is inclusive and consultative. Access of women to decision-making positions has not yet translated into pro-woman policies and laws. The lack of women in decision-making positions is a hindrance. Promoting gender equality can challenge patriarchal practices of societies and states; these can best be sorted by women. Therefore, women's involvement in peace processes would make a difference for the better. The role of concerned institutions in the post-conflict situations should include establishing priorities, ensuring gender equality, and coordinating with relevant stakeholders, rather than only delivering services.

Making visible unpaid care work may address the underlying context-specific constraints within which the basic services are implemented in order to be successful in the post-armed conflict settings. The most basic difficulty is the weak database and lack of gender disaggregated data. Gender disaggregated data is of crucial importance to the promotion of gender equality. Without reliable statistics, it is difficult to make a plea for activities that seek to combat inequality. Data disaggregated by gender are so far unavailable.

Africa has many more internally displaced persons (IDPs) than refugees—in 2010, there were around 2 million refugees and around 11 million IDPs. However, these numbers of the internally displaced in Africa are on the rise. Whenever there are new outbreaks of fighting, they create new waves of displacement. The share of children and women among IDPs is higher in Africa than elsewhere (Verwimp and Maystadt 2015). But while there is a 60-year-old convention on refugees and a dedicated UN agency to protect and assist refugees, the corresponding system for responding to internal displacement is much weaker (Ferris 2012). The vulnerability of the IDPs in Africa has certainly been overlooked for too long (Verwimp and Maystadt 2015). The African Union Convention for the Protection and Assistance of IDPs in Africa (Kampala Convention)[3] has entered into force since 2012. However, the question remains as to the actual impact of the Convention, if any. IDPs face harsh living conditions everywhere in Africa. Displacement remains arguably the most significant humanitarian challenge facing the world (Eweka and Olusegun 2016) and Africa in particular. Lack of appropriate basic care services has not so far been a cause for concern in IDP camps. In addition, the large influx of displaced people has placed a considerable strain on available basic care services. There is a severe shortage in drinking water and relief aid and terrible health services in the IDPs camps. There is still a gap between water demand and supply in the IDP camps. Temporal schools are made out of grass and twigs. Even though the government has managed to house war-affected populations in the IDP camps, the houses are so small to live in (10 × 10 meters).

To advance women's human rights concerns and access to justice requires more attention to the embodied experiences of care providers during and after wartime and to respond to their needs and priorities through appropriate measures. Specific attention to women's needs and priorities in conflict and post-conflict contexts, however, also requires the addressing of a range of historic and systemic gender gaps, unbalanced policies, and structures of discrimination, which have disadvantaged women (Goetz 2009). The harmonization of social policy around the four principles of care is much needed. The four care principles have just been conceived; therefore they have not yet been discussed and debated properly. This book strongly encourages African states to develop, enact, and update action plan as part of the State's responsibility to disseminate and implement the four principles of care on social well-being. Furthermore, there is a need to systematically evaluate and analyse the social and public policies and programs in place to assess their impacts on responding to women's care burden. This analysis could identify the gaps that are not addressed by these policies and programs that would guide future efforts.

Based on abovementioned, considering women as caregivers in a way that satisfies their needs is an essential step towards lasting peace in Africa as a whole. Yet the struggles and barriers that women face as caregivers/providers in post-conflict settings means that there is a need for institutionalizing and legitimizing women's empowerment in the policies and affirmative action. Supportive policies and allocated resources towards providing basic care services are essential for caregivers to continue providing quality care for their family and community alike. The capacities and capabilities of women as care providers during emergencies need to be taken into consideration in the rehabilitation planning in the aftermath of the conflict.

Notes

1. The Global Gender Gap Report 2015 is published by the World Economic Forum. http://reports.weforum.org/global-gender-gap-report-2015/.
2. UNAMID is the African Union/United Nations Hybrid *military operation* in *Darfur, which took over from the AU on 1st of January 2008.* https://unamid.unmissions.org/.
3. The African Union Convention for the Protection and Assistance of Internally Displaced Persons in Africa (Kampala Convention). https://au.int/sites/default/files/treaties/7796-treaty-003_kampala_convention_african_union_convention_for_the_protection_and_assistance_of_internally_displaced_persons_in_africa_e.pdf.

Bibliography

Akinboade, O.A. 2005. A Review of Women, Poverty and Informal Trade Issues in East and Southern Africa. *International Social Science Journal* 57 (184): 255–275.

Alaga, E. 2010. Challenges for Women in Peacebuilding in West Africa. Africa Institute of South Africa, Policy Briefs, AISA, June 2010, No. 18: 1–9.

Berry, M.E. 2018. *From Violence to Mobilization: War, Women, and Political Power in Rwanda and Bosnia-Herzegovina*. Cambridge: Cambridge University Press.

Budlender, D., and R. Moussié. 2013. *Making Care Visible: Women's Unpaid Care Work in Nepal, Nigeria, Uganda and Kenya*. Johannesburg: Action Aid. http://www.actionaid.org/sites/files/actionaid/making_care_visible.pdf.

Dodson, L., and J. Dickert. 2004. Girls' Family Labor in Low-Income Households: A Decade of Qualitative Research. *Journal of Marriage and Family* 66 (2): 318–332.

Domínguez-Serrano, M. 2012. Unpaid Care Work in Africa. Foundation BBVA, Working Papers Series, Working Paper, No. 6.

Elson, D. 2017. Recognize, Reduce, and Redistribute Unpaid Care Work: How to Close the Gender Gap. *New Labor Forum* 26 (2): 52–61.

Esquivel, V. 2014. What Is a Transformative Approach to Care, and Why Do We Need It? *Gender & Development* 22 (3): 423–439.

Esquivel, V. 2013. Care in Households and Communities: Background Paper on Conceptual Issues, Oxfam Research Report. ISBN: 978-1-78077-473-2.

Eweka, O., and T.O. Olusegun. 2016. Management of Internally Displaced Persons in Africa: Comparing Nigeria and Cameroon. *Africa Research Review, An International Multidisciplinary Journal* 10 (1): 193–210. Published online January 2016. https://dx.doi.org/10.4314/afrrev.v10i1.15.

Fälth, A., and M. Blackden. 2009. Unpaid Care Work. Gender Equality and Poverty Reduction Policy Brief, Issue 1, UNDP, New York.

Ferris, E. 2012. *Internal Displacement in Africa: An Overview of Trends and Opportunities*, 1–12. New York: Brookings-LSE Project on Internal Displacement.

Fraser, N. 2007. Feminist Politics in the Age of Recognition: A Two-Dimensional Approach to Gender Justice. *Studies in Social Justice* 1 (1): 23–35.

Friedman, M. 2009. Review of Daniel Engster, The Heart of Justice: Care Ethics and Political Theory. *The Philosophical Review* 118 (2): 256–258.

Goetz, A.M. 2009. UNIFEM Issue Brief: Promoting Gender Equality in Recovery and Peacebuilding: Planning and Financing, Monitoring and Accountability.

Haggaz, A.A., E.A. Radi, and I. Adam. 2007. High Maternal Mortality in Darfur, Sudan. *International Journal of Gynecology and Obstetrics* 98 (3): 252–268.

Himmelweit, S., and A. Plomien. 2014. Feminist Perspectives on Care: Theory, Practice and Policy. In *The Sage Handbook of Feminist Theory*, ed. Mary Evans, Clare Hemmings, Marsha Henry, Hazel Johnstone, Sumi Madhok, Ania Plomien, and Sadie Wearing, 446–464. London: Sage.

Krause, J., W. Krause, and P. Bränfors. 2018. Women's Participation in Peace Negotiations and the Durability of Peace. *International Interactions* 44 (6): 985–1016. Published Online 10 August 2018. http://dx.doi.org/10.1080/03050629.2018.1492386.

Kröger, T. 2009. Care Research and Disability Studies: Nothing in Common? *Critical Social Policy* 29 (3): 398–420.

Landers, C. 2009. Maternal and Newborn Health: A Global Challenge. US Fund for UNICEF Youth Report. Available at http://youth.unicefusa.org/assets/pdf/0027-unicef-youthreport09-8_4.pdf.

Maestre, M., and J. Thorpe. 2016, May. *Understanding Unpaid Care Work to Empower Women in Market Systems Approaches*. London: The BEAM Exchange. Retrieved from https://www.beamexchange.org.

Morrison, A., D. Raju, and N. Sinha. 2007. Gender Equality, Poverty and Economic Growth. World Bank, Gender and Development Group. The World Bank, Policy Research Working Paper 4349.

Naraghi-Anderlini, S. 2006. Mainstreaming Gender in Conflict Analysis: Issues and Recommendations. Social Development Papers on Conflict Prevention and Reconstruction, No. 32. World Bank.

Razavi, S. 2007. The Political and Social Economy of Care in a Development Context: Conceptual Issues, Research Questions and Policy Options. Gender and Development, Paper No. 3. UNRISD, Geneva.

Sen, A. 1999. *Development as Freedom*. New York: Alfred A. Knopf.

Sevenhuijsen, S., V. Bozalek, A. Gouws, and M. Minnar-McDonald. 2003. South African Social Welfare Policy: An Analysis Using the Ethic of Care. *Critical Social Policy* 23 (3): 299–321.

Thompson, M.E., M.S. Toro, and K.A. Gómez. 2007. Feminist Media Coverage of Women in War: 'You Are Our Eyes and Ears to the World'. *Gender & Development* 15 (3): 435–450.

Tubiana, J., V. Tanner, and M.A. Abdul-Jalil. 2012. *Traditional Authorities' Peacemaking Role in Darfur*. Washington, DC: United States Institute of Peace (USIP).

UNFPA—United Nations Population Fund. 2001. The Impact of Armed Conflict on Women and Girls a Consultative Meeting on Mainstreaming Gender in Areas of Conflict and Reconstruction. https://www.unfpa.org/sites/default/files/pub-pdf/impact_conflict_women.pdf.

UN—United Nations. 2017. Final Report of the UN High-Level Panel on Women's Economic Empowerment Calls on "Leave No One Behind: Taking Action for Transformational Change on Women's Economic Empowerment". New York, NY: United Nations Headquarters. http://www.unwomen.org/en/news/stories/2017/3/new-final-report-of-the-un-high-levelpanel-on-womens-economic-empowerment.

UN—United Nations. 2013. Extreme Poverty and Human Rights: Unpaid Care Work and Women's Human Rights. Sepulveda Carmona, M. The Special Rapporteur's Report to the 68th Session of the General Assembly (A/68/293).

Verwimp, P., and J.-F. Maystadt. 2015. Forced Displacement and Refugees in Sub-Saharan Africa: An Economic Inquiry. Policy Research Working Paper, No. 7517, World Bank, Washington, DC.

Zachorowska-Mazurkiewicz, A. 2015. The Concept of Care in Institutional and Feminist Economics and Its Impact on Public Policy. *Journal of Economic* 49 (2): 405–413.

Zuckerman, E., and M. Greenberg. 2004. The Gender Dimensions of Post-conflict Reconstruction: An Analytical Framework for Policymakers. *Gender and Development* 12 (3): 70–82.

Index

F. O. Ibnouf, *War-Time Care Work and Peacebuilding in Africa*, Gender, Development and Social Change,
https://doi.org/10.1007/978-3-030-26195-5

Printed by Printforce, the Netherlands